Delta|Academic|Objectives

Reading skills

Louis Rogers

DELTA Publishing
Quince Cottage
Hoe Lane
Peaslake
Surrey GU5 9SW
England

www.deltapublishing.co.uk

First published 2011

Edited by Catriona Watson-Brown
Designed by Caroline Johnston
Cartoons by CartoonStock (pages 25,
35, 55, 73, 90, 104)
Photos by iStock (pages 23, 27, 44b, 48,
54, 107) and Shutterstock (pages 9, 11,
14, 18a Atlaspix/Shutterstock.com, 18b
3777190317/Shutterstock.com, 18c Filip
Fuxa/Shutterstock.com, 18d Helga
Esteb/Shutterstock.com, 31, 42, 44a, 44c,
59, 64, 68, 79, 82, 85, 99, 101)
Cover design by Peter Bushell
Printed in Malta by Melita Press

ISBN Book 978-1-905085-56-9

Author acknowledgements

I would like to thank various people for their help in the development of this book. In particular, I would like to thank Emma Kuhles, Nashwa Nashaat, Diane Schmitt and Liz Wilding for their valuable feedback. I would also like to thank Val Baker, Dawn Clarke, Prue Griffiths and Clare Nukui for the valuable discussions and input. For taking the time to meet with me and discuss the concept, I would like to thank Philip Lodge, Mary Mayall, Asmaa Awad, Dr Siddig and William Vize. Thank you to the many people at DELTA publishing for their help the development of this book. For all the editorial support and feedback, I would like to thank Catriona Watson-Brown. For the fantastic design work, Caroline Johnston. From developing the concept to helping push it forward to the product it is, I would like to thank Nick Boisseau and Chris Hartley. I would also especially like to thank my wife, Cathy Rogers, for all her support and patience during the writing.

Text acknowledgements

We are grateful to the following for permission to reproduce copyright material:

Taylor & Francis for an extract from *The Student Assessment Handbook*, by Dunn, L., Morgan, C., O'Reilly, M. and Parry, S. 2006, pp.15–16, copyright © Taylor & Francis, 2006; Guardian News & Media Ltd for an extract from 'How many resits is too much' by Sheppard, J., *The Guardian*, 3rd August 2009, copyright © Guardian News & Media Ltd, 2009; Cengage Learning, Inc. for an extract from *The Leadership Experience*, 4th edition by Daft, R., 2008, pp.5–8, copyright © 2008, South-Western, a part of Cengage Learning, Inc. Reproduced by permission. www.cengage.com/permissions; Education, Audiovisual and Culture Executive Agency (EACEA) for an extract from *Key Data on Teaching Languages at School in Europe*, 2008 edition, p.34, http://eacea.ec.europa.eu, copyright © Education, Audiovisual and Culture Executive Agency, 2008; Multilingual Matters for an extract from *Early Learning of Modern Foreign Languages: Processes and outcomes*, eds Nikolov, M., Multilingual Matters, 2009, copyright © Multilingual Matters; The Worldwatch Institute for extracts from 'Reducing work time as a path to sustainability' by John de Graaf and 'Editing out unsustainable behaviour' by Maniates, M., published in *State of the World 2010: Transforming Cultures from Consumerism to Sustainability*, pp.173–177 and 119–120, www.worldwatch.org, copyright © The Worldwatch Institute; Cengage Learning EMEA for an extract from *Criminology: Theories, Patterns and Typologies, 10th edition* by Siegel, L., 2010, pp.130–132, copyright © Cengage Learning EMEA; Polity Press for an extract from *Sociology* by Giddens, A., 2006, pp.800–802. Copyright © Polity Press; Pearson Education Ltd for extracts from *Management* by Boddy, D., 2008, pp.130–132; and *Management and Organisational Behaviour* by Mullins, L.J. 2005, p.556–559, copyright © Pearson Education Ltd; Cengage Learning EMEA for an extract from *Business Ethics 2009 Update: Ethical Decision-Making and Cases, 7th edition* by Ferrell, O.C., Fraedrich, J. and Ferrell, L., 2009, pp.124–126, copyright © Cengage Learning EMEA; John Wiley & Sons Ltd for extracts from *Consumer Behaviour* by Evans, M., Jamal, A., and Foxhall, G. 2006, pp.108–113. Reproduced with permission of John Wiley & Sons Ltd; Oxford University Press for two figures of data from 'Dietary quality in relationship to ten-year mortality in older Europeans: The SENECA Study' by Haveman-Nies, A., Lisette, P.G.M., de Groot, J.B., Amorim Cruz, J.A., Osler, M. and van Staveren, W.A., *American Journal of Epidemiology*, 156, pp.962–968. 2002. Copyright © 2002, Oxford University Press; and University of California Press for an extract from *Damned lies and statistics: untangling numbers from the media, politicians, and activists* by Best, J., 2001, p.13, copyright © University of California Press, permission conveyed through Copyright Clearance Center.

In some instances we have been unable to trace the owners of copyright material and we would appreciate any information that would enable us to do so.

Contents

using the text	critical thinking	language focus
Selecting texts	Identifying stance	1 Selecting vocabulary 2 Identifying features of formal writing
Selecting information	Questions to analyze texts	1 The Academic Word List 2 Dictionary skills – meaning and context
Summarizing	Fact and opinion	1 Tense review – past and present simple 2 Common suffixes
Paraphrasing	Reasons and conclusions	1 Prefixes 2 Dictionary skills – word form
Discussing texts	Cause and connection	1 Modals and hedging 2 Alternative and counter-arguments
Integrating ideas	Bias, expertise and neutrality	1 Connected ideas 2 Pronoun referents
Direct quotes	Interpreting the criticisms of others	1 Noun collocations 2 Noun phrases
Indirect quotes	Persuasive language	1 Active vs. passive 2 Verb collocations
Summarizing from multiple sources	Evaluating evidence	1 Comparison and contrast 2 Reporting
Bibliographies and references	Statistics	1 Cause and effect 2 Describing graphs

Introduction

Whilst understanding the basic meaning of an academic text is a challenge, so is understanding an argument, assessing the strength of it or even its validity. Once you have understood it, what do you do with it? How do you incorporate these ideas with others and your own? This book forms part of the *Delta Academic Objectives* series that will help you to adapt to the challenges of studying academically in the English language.

The texts

Most of the texts in this book are from original academic textbooks and are similar in style to those you may come across in your studies. They cover a wide range of subject areas, including some of the most commonly found disciplines in academic study. You do not have to be a specialist in the field to study these texts, as the topics are both academic and common to everyday life.

Aims

This book aims to prepare you for the challenges of reading academically. Unlike in general English, where you often simply have to understand the general meaning of a text, in academic reading you are expected to do much more with what you read. This book prepares you for this by covering four main areas.

- **Understanding the text**

  Comprehension of the text remains essential, and it is important that you also analyze the text by asking questions such as:
  - Is this text useful?
  - What is the main idea?
  - What is the author's point of view?
  - What unspoken arguments or conclusions are behind this text?

- **Critical thinking**

  One of the key challenges you will face when reading academic texts is to engage critically with the academic community. This involves not simply accepting ideas that are written but learning to constantly challenge and question the ideas of others. You need to ask yourself questions such as:
  - Is this argument logical?
  - What evidence is there?
  - What weaknesses are there in the argument?
  - How is the author trying to persuade the reader?

- **Using the text**

  In general English, it is quite common to write without any need to support your opinion. However, in academic writing, you will, in most cases, be expected to strengthen and support your opinion using your research. It can help to think about points such as:
  - Which part of the text best supports my opinion?
  - How can I put this into my own words?
  - How can I show this is another person's idea?
  - How can I include it in my essay?'
  This skill is also practised further in the companion book, *Delta Academic Objectives: Writing skills*.

● **Language focus**

Reading should not only be seen as a step to understanding the text and using it in your writing. It is also a key method for learning and developing your vocabulary. By developing your knowledge of lexis typical of academic texts, you will not only be able to understand a wider range of texts but also start to transfer this knowledge into your writing. This section will help you to develop these skills and think about points such as:

– What vocabulary should I learn?
– Should I learn the word or a whole phrase?
– How does this vocabulary connect ideas in the text?

This skill is also practised further in the companion book, *Delta Academic Objectives: Writing skills.*

How to use this book

There are 12 units in this book: ten of these each covers a different theme, and the other two (Units 6 and 12) are revision units, giving you the chance to review what you have learned. The main units do not have to be studied in order – you can use the contents grid on pages 4 and 5 to select the areas or topics that you feel are of most use or interest to you. However, it is advisable to study whole units and not just particular sections, as the exercises in the different sections are often interrelated. The revision units relate to the skills areas covered in the preceding five units, so it is a good idea to ensure that you have done all five units before tackling the revision exercises.

The Academic Word List (AWL)

In line with the theme of language development, the AWL is also a feature of this book (see Unit 2 for more details). At the end of the book are 12 pages (one for each unit) with exercises to test some of the vocabulary in the AWL. These can be done at any time and subsequently revisited to check what you have remembered. These are followed by the 570 headwords that make up the AWL, provided for easy reference.

1 Education

Aims

- Identifying the purpose and audience of a text
- Selecting vocabulary to learn
- Selecting texts for further reading
- Identifying a writer's stance
- Identifying features of formal writing

Topic focus

1 Think about and write down three things you:

- remember about school;
- liked about school;
- disliked about school.

2 Work with a partner. Discuss these questions.

1 What is the main purpose of education?

2 What have you enjoyed most about your education so far?

3 What is the most difficult experience you have had in education?

4 What is your opinion on tests and assessment?

3 Look at these opinions on education. Who might have these opinions (e.g. teachers, parents, students, politicians, etc.), and why? Which ones match your own?

1 I didn't like coursework at school – I preferred exams.

2 Assessment is important in maintaining the standards of education.

3 People are judged throughout their life; assessment is just another form of this.

4 Effective teaching is key to student learning.

5 We could not have confidence in the standard of education without government checks.

6 Teaching needs to be informative and interesting.

7 Education is mainly about getting a job afterwards.

Study tip
When you write an academic essay, opinions need to be supported and informed by your own research and reading. Very few academic essays are written using only your own opinion. You will look at how to select texts to use in your essays in the *Using the text* section (page 13).

4 Imagine somebody wanted to support one of the opinions in Exercise 3. What evidence would they need to find to support each one?

Pre-reading

1 Look at the images above, then complete this table. Can you think of any other types of publication? What are their purposes?

type of publication	purpose(s) of the publication
novel	to entertain

2 Look at the book titles below (a–d) and discuss these questions with a partner.

1 Who might be interested in reading the book?

Example: **a** This would be of interest to English teachers, testing experts, governments, etc.

2 Is it possible from the title to guess the purpose of the book?

Example: **a** We know it is about assessment of English in an academic situation. However, we cannot be sure if it is aimed at undergraduates/postgraduates learning about assessment, writers of assessments, or students preparing to be assessed, etc.

a

Assessing English for Academic Purposes

b

Innovative assessment in higher education

c

THE STUDENT ASSESSMENT HANDBOOK

d

The International Student's Survival Guide:
How to get the most from studying at a UK university

3 **When selecting a text for use in an essay, you have to consider a number of things, for example who the author is and what their purpose for writing is. Discuss these questions with a partner.**

1 Why is it important to consider who the author is?

2 Why do you have to consider the writer's purpose?

3 Why do you have to consider the audience the text is written for?

4 **Quickly read the two texts, below and on page 11, and discuss these questions with a partner.**

1 What is the purpose of each text, e.g. to persuade, inform, explain, evaluate, describe, etc.?

2 Where would you expect to find such a text, e.g. journal, textbook, newspaper, blog?

3 Who might be interested in reading each text, and why?

Text A

Roles and purpose of assessment

The question of why students are assessed might at first seem to be simple common sense; it is obvious that their performance needs to be measured. Looking a little further, it may be that the assessment of students has followed subject traditions or regulatory requirements. As a result, teachers have not had the need or luxury of time to wonder too much about why an approach was adopted. But assessment tasks and strategies vary enormously, both across and within different subjects. To be able to make informed decisions about how to assess students, teachers have to take into account the roles and purposes of student assessment. When we consider that the assessment of learning is of interest to a range of different people, we can also see that the processes and outcomes of assessment can address a number of different needs.

Maintaining standards

For example, our society expects universities and colleges to uphold standards of excellence in learning. In its turn, the institution is interested in assessment of students in order to maintain standards and its reputation. Individual institutions must meet the needs of their communities. The apparently successful achievement of its graduates ensures an institution's programmes remain attractive to prospective students, also for those who return to study for higher degrees or to gain additional qualifications. Professional groups might be interested in assessment practices to ensure standards in the profession.

Students – the primary stakeholders?

In considering stakeholders in the assessment process, we must consider the main stakeholders – students themselves. The principal aim of assessment, from the students' perspective, is to improve the quality of student learning. According to Biggs (1999b:68), 'assessment in practice has two functions: to tell us whether or not the learning has been successful; also to convey to students what we want them to learn'. Unfortunately, when we investigate the experiences of assessment that students remember, we often find many horror stories of learning by dislike. The assessment tasks that were difficult for students to handle or that stopped their efforts to learn are the lasting ones in the minds of students. As a result, they promise to keep away from such subject areas or such assessment methods forever.

Almost one in ten sixth-formers who take French AS-Level – the first year of A-level – resit a unit more than twice. Furthermore, over half retake one more than once, the exams watchdog Ofqual has found. Just how many resits should be allowed? Far fewer than currently take place, according to Lord Sutherland, the head of a government inquiry into testing. Lord Sutherland said today that at the moment there is 'capacity for re-entry and re-entry and re-entry, particularly at AS-level. I don't think that is a very sensible way of assessing a student's performance'.

The maximum number of resits by any one student is six. Ofqual has calculated that the percentage of A grades would fall from 25.3% to 21.6% if resits were banned. Lord Sutherland, who is also chair of the exam markers and assessors' body, said: 'Obviously, you have to have a system to allow people who are ill on the day or disadvantaged for other reasons to

apply for a resit. But you have to be very careful with these requests. I can remember a student who claimed his third grandmother had died.'

Ofqual says there is strong support from teachers, head teachers and students for reducing the number of resits at AS-Level. Some teachers told the watchdog they felt they had no choice but to encourage their students to resit units, even if they did not think it was necessary.

Check your comprehension

5 Read Text A again and answer these questions.

1 Choose the correct option about the role of assessment.
   a The author thinks that the only role of assessment is to measure performance.
   b The author thinks that the role of assessment is to meet the needs of a number of different people.

2 Choose the correct option about assessment methods.
   a The author thinks that assessment methods are quite old and traditional.
   b The author thinks that assessment methods are regularly changed by teachers.

3 Why does the author think universities are interested in assessment?

4 What will be the benefit for universities if its graduates are successful?

5 According to the author, the main aim of assessment for students is 'to improve the quality of learning'. Does the author think this happens in reality?

6 Does the author's opinion in the final lines match your own experience?

6 Read Text B again and answer these questions.

1 How many students resit one unit more than once?

2 Does Lord Sutherland believe resits are a good idea?

3 When does he think resits are acceptable?

4 Do teachers agree that fewer resits should be allowed?

5 How does your country's approach to resits compare to this situation?

Language focus 1: selecting vocabulary

1 Discuss these questions with a partner.

  1 Do you need to understand all the words in a text to understand the overall meaning?

  2 What can you do if you do not understand a word?

  3 How do you decide what vocabulary is important to learn?

  4 What do you think is the most effective method for learning vocabulary?

2 a **Look back at the texts in this unit and highlight the words you did not know.**

  b **Discuss with a partner whether you think these words are important to learn. How did you decide?**

  c **Which of the words you highlighted might be useful for an essay on the topic of assessment?**

  d **Which other words might be useful for an essay on this topic?**

Learning vocabulary **3** **What does it mean to *know* a word? Discuss with a partner what else you need to know besides the meaning of a word.**

4 **Add to this table using words from Exercise 2. Your ideas from Exercise 3 can go in the blank columns.**

word formation	example sentence	translations		
assess (v.) assessment (n.) assessed (adj.)	The main aim of education is to assess students' ability in a subject.			

The Academic Word List

 Some vocabulary is common in academic writing and can be used in any academic subject (physics, economics, maths, law, etc.). The words in Exercise 5 are taken from the Academic Word List. You will learn more about this in Unit 2.

5 Look at the academic vocabulary (1–8) and match each word to its more informal equivalent (a–h). Use a dictionary where necessary.

  1 assume   **a** idea

  2 concept   **b** come from

  3 constitute   **c** give out

  4 derive   **d** clear

  5 distribute   **e** important

  6 evident   **f** believe

  7 significant   **g** make up

  8 interpret   **h** understand

Focusing your research

1 Look at the mind map below related to this essay question. What main topics would you expect to find in this student's essay?

> **Study tip**
> It can be challenging to select useful and relevant materials efficiently. Making use of book titles, contents pages, indexes and subheadings can help efficient and effective text selection.

> Too much testing affects learning negatively. Discuss.

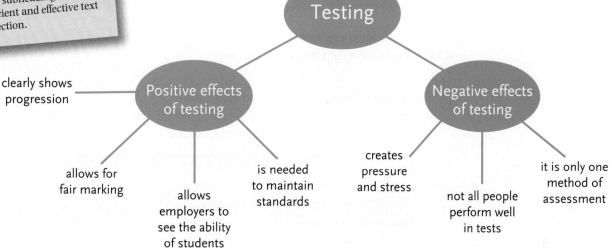

2 a Look at this essay question and check the meaning of any unknown words.

> Self- and peer assessment lead to unfair and inaccurate marking. Discuss.

b Answer these questions.

1 Is peer or self-assessment common in your country?

2 Have you ever taken part in peer assessment?

3 Which of these books (1–3) do you think would contain useful information to answer the essay question in Exercise 2?

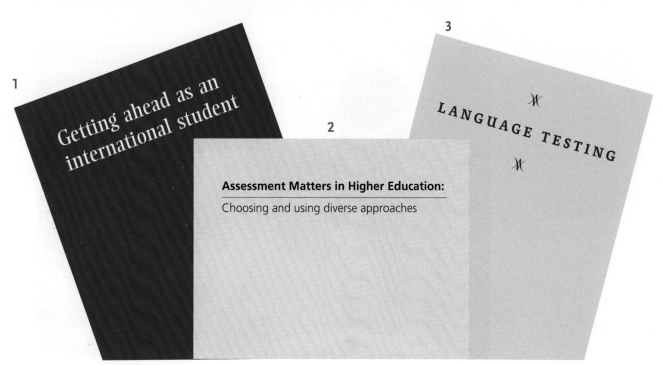

4 These are the four main sections (a–d) of one of the books in Exercise 3. Which section(s) would be the most useful for the essay question in Exercise 2?

a **Approaches to assessment**

b **Exploring the effectiveness of innovative assessment**

c **Assessing practice**

d **Towards autonomous assessment**

5 These are the headings from three chapters (i–iii) of the same book. Which chapter(s) might be useful, and why?

i

What are self-assessment and peer assessment?

Why is there so much interest in the use of self-assessment and peer assessment?

How are we to understand the many approaches?

ii

Previous module and assessment structure

Motivation for changes

The new structure

The peer-assessment process

Benefits of the peer-assessment exercise

Negative effects of the peer-assessment exercise

iii

Setting up the exercise

Letting go of ownership

Student discussions on criteria of assessment

Student self-selection of groups and selection of topics

The presentations, the 'post-mortem' discussions and the award of grades

The grades awarded

Critical thinking: identifying stance

Identifying main opinion 1 **Look again at the essay question from Exercise 1 in the last section. What is the opinion in each of the sentences below (1–4) in relation to this question? Which present arguments for, and which against?**

> Too much testing affects learning negatively. Discuss.

1 'When teachers share with their students the process of assessment – giving up control, sharing power and leading students to take on the authority to assess themselves – the professional judgement of both is enhanced.' (Brew, 1999)

2 'Stefani (1994) discusses some of the concerns of lecturers of handing over control of assessment to students, with the main concern being that marks might differ from those awarded by the teacher. This study found that there may be some concern here.' (Lapham and Webster, 1999)

3 '"Much of the literature on self-assessment and peer assessment is devoted to the issue of whether students' assessment is in line with teacher." This obsession with comparing the marks given by each is perhaps surprising, given the ease with which it is frequently assumed that two teachers would come up with the same mark.' (Piper et al., 1996)

4 'Students' inability to judge themselves and peers objectively was a concern. Also common was an inability to distinguish between effort and quality of output.' (Jordan, 1999)

2 **Look at the essay on page 16, written in response to the question in Exercise 1, and answer these questions.**

1 Does the writer agree or disagree with the essay question? How do you know this?

2 How have they supported their arguments?

3 Are there any weaknesses in the arguments?

4 What language is used to present arguments? Underline examples. (One has been done for you.)

Evaluating arguments 3 **Work with a partner. Write suggestions to the author of the essay in Exercise 2 on how the essay can be improved. Focus on:**

● strength of argument;

● strength of evidence;

● conclusions reached.

Incorporating arguments 4 **Look at these statements with a partner and decide whether each of them is true (T) or false (F).**

1 It is common to write academic essays based on personal opinion only.

2 Using other academic sources strengthens your essay's argument.

3 Reading should inform your opinion.

4 You may need to revise your opinion after reading.

Study tip
It is important to let your reading influence your opinion. Do not stay with your original line of argument if your research has shown that there are stronger arguments for the opposite side.

5 **Look back at the opinions in Exercise 1. Which ones match the stance the author of the article has taken? Which ones contradict it?**

Assessment is central to almost all forms of education around the world, and in recent years, a wider variety of assessment has tended to be used. One such form of this change is the use of peer and self-assessment. Self-assessment can be defined as 'the ability to critically assess one's own work' (Brew, 1999: 160) and peer assessment as 'making judgements about, or commenting upon, each other's work' (Brew, 1999: 160). As with all assessment methods, these two both have their own strengths and weaknesses. It can be argued that peer and self-assessment with careful initiation and moderation are effective methods of assessment. However, this essay will argue that in the high-stakes environments of most educational settings, these methods are inappropriate, as the marking is unreliable.

Peer and self-assessment have become increasingly common as methods of assessment, particularly in further and higher education. They are used as methods to reduce the marking loads of teachers and, it is claimed, to enhance group work and the critical thinking skills of students. It is also claimed that if marking criteria are discussed and agreed at the start, students' marking does not differ significantly from teachers'. In studies where the assessment of different teachers is compared, and also in studies where teacher and peer and or self-assessments are compared, it has generally been found that, provided criteria are discussed and agreed in advance, marks tend to be similar (Boud and Falchikov, 1989). Thus it could be argued that with the right initial training, there is no difference between work being marked by a teacher or a student.

However, it is debatable as to whether students will mark in the same way as a teacher. There are issues with students collaborating to give agreed marks, bias towards friendship groups, and the commitment and dedication of all individuals concerned. A study by Lapham and Webster (1999) on a third-year module of 60 management students in Thames Valley University found that collaboration, bias and a lack of seriousness was a concern for a number of students. Therefore, peer and self-assessment can be said to be unreliable, as the students are not independent and professional in the same manner as a teacher.

In conclusion, peer and self-assessment are increasingly common and are likely to be encountered by numerous students in further and higher education. It has been argued that peer and self-assessment differ little from teacher assessment in terms of the marks awarded. However, it is clear that issues with collaboration, bias and commitment far outweigh any advantages. These weaknesses will clearly, therefore, lead to inaccurate and unfair marking of students' work, and alternative more suitable methods need to be introduced.

Language focus 2: identifying features of formal writing

Identifying language

1 a **Look at these sentences. The second one is more formal than the first. Why is that?**

    1 A lot of people have got jobs in my country at the moment.

    2 The UK currently has high levels of unemployment.

b **What other features of formal writing can you think of?**

2 **Look at these two texts. Which one is more formal?**

Text A

Assessment probably provokes more anxiety among students and irritation among staff than any other feature of higher education. It occupies a great deal of time that might otherwise be devoted to teaching and learning, and it is the subject of considerable debate about whether it is fair, effective and worth spending so much effort on.

Text B

Tests are for future employees and tutors to know that you've a basic knowledge of the subject. If you can do well at GCSE chemistry without knowing much about chemistry, they might as well distribute the blank certificates for you to fill your name in. I loved science and am now a research scientist; everyone should be encouraged to study science, but it's fair to say that it doesn't suit everybody.

3 **This table shows some of the features of academic writing. Look at the texts in this unit. Find more examples of features of academic writing and add them to the table.**

cautious (hedging) language *may perhaps be*	**passive voice** *students are assessed*
noun + noun combination *assessment tasks*	**noun + *of* + noun** *assessment of students*
relative clauses *that students remember*	**linking adverbs / adverbial phrases** *as a result*
tenses Present simple: *vary enormously*	

Using language

4 **Use phrases using 'noun + *of* + noun' to write three sentences about education.**

Example: Seminars are a <u>feature of higher education</u> in the UK.

Unit extension

1 **Look at this essay question. Type the word *education* into a search engine and look for books on this topic.**

> Education should be about knowledge and learning, not about getting a good job. Discuss.

2 **Select two or three books you feel are relevant. Look at the contents page of each. Which book(s) and which chapter(s) would be most useful? Why? Bring the name of the books and chapters to the next class. Explain to a partner why you chose the book(s) and chapter(s).**

2 Leadership

Aims

- Practising skimming and scanning for information
- Discovering the Academic Word List
- Developing questions to analyze texts
- Selecting information to use in writing
- Using dictionaries to understand meaning from context

Topic focus

1 Look at the different leaders in the pictures above and think about these questions.

　1　Who do you think is/was more important? Why?

　2　Are there any similarities between the role of each person?

2 Work with a partner and discuss these questions.

　1　Have you ever been in a leadership role or been led by somebody? Describe the experience.

　2　What do you think makes an effective leader? List five qualities of a good leader.

　3　Are different leadership skills needed in different jobs or roles?

　4　How would you define leadership?

3 a Look at this essay question on leadership and underline the key words.

> Changes to modern society mean that effective leaders from the past would no longer be effective today. Discuss.

　b Work with a partner and brainstorm your own ideas on this topic.

　c Write questions that will help you research this topic. Think about the specific information you would need to answer this question.

Understanding the text: skimming vs. scanning

> ℹ Skimming and scanning are used to look through a text quickly. Scanning is used when you are looking for a specific piece of information, for example, using reading lists, bibliographies, contents pages and tables to find specific information. Skimming is used to try to quickly understand the general sense of a passage. This skill is used when you have a specific question in mind such as 'Is this passage useful to answer the essay question?', 'What is the writer's opinion?', 'What is the purpose?'.

Scanning

1 Cameron and Green (2008) identified five key roles used by effective leaders. These roles are known as: Thoughtful Architect (TA), Tenacious Implementer (TI), Measured Connector (MC), Visionary Motivator (VM) and Edgy Catalyzer (EC). Look at the three graphs below and answer these questions.

Study tip
You have had some brief practice of this in Unit 1 (pages 13–14) to identify useful books, chapters and subheadings whilst researching. You will now use the same skill to quickly find information in the charts in this section.

1 Which graph shows people's views of themselves as leaders?

2 Which graph shows people's views of leadership in their organization?

3 Which is the most common style in people's organizations?

4 Which is the least common style in people's organizations?

5 Which role do people most see themselves like?

6 Which role would people least like to be led by?

7 A natural Tenacious Implementer would prefer to have what kind of role?

8 A Thoughtful Architect would prefer to have what kind of role?

a) You as a leader

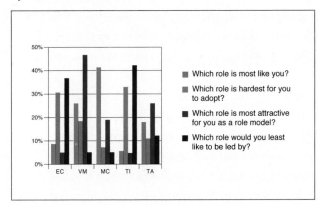

b) Leadership in your organization

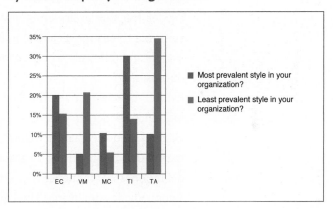

c) Natural role and preferred role

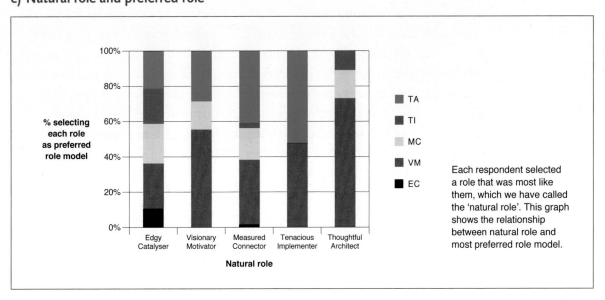

Each respondent selected a role that was most like them, which we have called the 'natural role'. This graph shows the relationship between natural role and most preferred role model.

2 Look at the text below and answer these questions.

1 What is the text about?

Study tip
You have had some brief practice of this reading skill in Unit 1, page 10.

2 How many points does leadership involve?

3 Which points are detailed in paragraph 2?

4 Which points are detailed in paragraph 3?

5 What's the main idea in paragraph 4?

Detailed understanding **3 Check your understanding by answering these questions.**

1 Which of these statements best matches the author's opinion on leadership?
  a A leader controls people.
  b Leaders influence people and are influenced by people.
  c Threats are the best way to control people.

2 Who decides on the changes needed in a situation?

3 When can a scientist be considered a leader?

4 Are leaders and followers considered different?

5 What are the qualities of a good follower?

Definition of leadership

Leadership studies are an emerging discipline, and the concept of leadership will continue to change. Leadership here is defined as an influence relationship among leaders and followers who want real changes and outcomes that reflect their shared purposes.

Exhibit 1.1 summarizes the key elements in this definition. Leadership involves influence, it occurs among people, those people intentionally desire significant changes, and the changes reflect purposes shared by leaders and followers. *Influence* means that the relationship among people is not passive; however, also part of this definition is that influence is multidirectional. It does not use orders or threats to make somebody do something. The basic cultural values in North America make it easiest to think of leadership as something a leader does to a follower. However, leadership has an effect in both directions. In most organizations, superiors influence subordinates, but subordinates also influence superiors. The people involved in the relationship want real and important changes – leadership involves creating change, not maintaining what normally happens. In addition, the changes sought are not dictated by leaders, but reflect purposes that leaders and followers share. Moreover, change is toward an outcome that leader and follower both want; a desired future or shared purpose that motivates them toward this more preferable outcome. An important aspect of leadership is influencing others to come together around a common vision. Thus, leadership involves the influence of people to bring about change toward a desirable future.

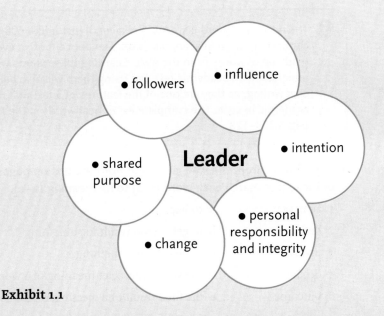

Exhibit 1.1

Also, leadership is a people activity and is separate and different from administrative paperwork and planning activities. Leadership occurs *among* people; it is not something done *to* people. Since leadership involves people, there must be followers. An individual performer who achieves excellence as a scientist, musician, athlete may be a leader in their field of expertise. However, they are not leaders as defined in this book unless followers are involved. Followers are an important part of the leadership process, and all leaders are sometimes followers as well. Good leaders know how to follow, and they set an example for others. The issue of intention, or will, means that people – leaders and followers – are actively involved in the pursuit of change. Each person takes personal responsibility to achieve the desired future.

One stereotype is that leaders are somehow different, that they are above others. However, in reality, the qualities needed for effective leadership are the same as those needed to be an effective follower. Effective followers think for themselves and carry out assignments with energy and enthusiasm. They are committed to something outside their own self-interest and have courage to protect what they believe. Good followers are not 'yes people' who blindly follow a leader. Effective leaders and effective followers may sometimes be the same person, playing different roles at different times. At its best, leadership is shared among leaders and followers, with everyone fully engaged and accepting higher levels of responsibility.

Language focus 1: the Academic Word List

 The Academic Word List (AWL) is a list of just under 600 words that are commonly found in academic texts. Ten per cent of an average academic text is made up of words from the AWL. Learning these words will clearly help you to understand an academic text, but using them will also help to formalize your own writing, as they are one of the features of a text that make it sound more academic in style. The complete list of headwords in the AWL appears on pages 123–128.

1 **These words from the AWL are taken from the text on pages 20–21. Use the context of the text to match each word (1–5) to its meaning (a–e).**

1 achieve	**a** to happen
2 define	**b** to get a good result in something
3 involve	**c** to be part of something
4 occur	**d** to explain the exact meaning of a word or idea
5 outcome	**e** the final result of a meeting, discussion, etc.

2 **Complete the sentences below using the words in the box.**

achievements	defined	involves	occur	outcome

1 Leadership can be .... as the quality of being good at leading a group.
2 One of his best .... was his successful management of the merger.
3 Unfortunately, the .... was not what he had wanted.
4 Academic writing usually .... undertaking research.
5 The meetings .... every two weeks.

3 **Complete this table with the correct related forms of the verbs.**

verb	noun	adjective	adverb
achieve	1	2	
define	3	4	5 ....
involve	6	7	
focus	8	9	
occur	10		

4 **Select two of the words from Exercise 3 and use them to write your own sentences.**

Example: The project involved a focused study of the data.

 On pages 111–122 are 12 sets of exercises related to the Academic Word List. The items practised are those that most commonly occur in each unit and/or are most closely linked to the theme of the unit. Take a look and do the exercises related to Unit 1.

Critical thinking: questions to analyze texts

> ℹ️ The first stage in analyzing a text, which we looked at in Unit 1, is to identify its main purpose and the audience it is aimed at. To focus your reading, it can then be useful to have some questions in mind related to an essay or the topic in general.

1 **Work with a partner and use these topics to write questions that help you analyze a text.**

- main point
- supporting idea
- argument
- evidence
- assumption
- bias
- facts
- opinions
- organization
- definitions

Examples:

What are the arguments the author uses to support their main point?

Is the argument logical?

2 a **Look at this extract from the text on page 21 and use the questions you wrote in Exercise 1 to analyze it.**

… leadership is a people activity and is separate and different from administrative paperwork and planning activities. Leadership occurs *among* people; it is not something done *to* people. Since leadership involves people, there must be followers. An individual performer who achieves excellence as a scientist, musician, athlete may be a leader in their field of expertise. However, they are not leaders as defined in this book unless followers are involved. Followers are an important part of the leadership process, and all leaders are sometimes followers as well. Good leaders know how to follow, and they set an example for others. The issue of intention, or will, means that people – leaders and followers – are actively involved in the pursuit of change. Each person takes personal responsibility to achieve the desired future.

b **Compare your answers with a partner.**

3 a **Look back at the text on pages 20–21 and use your questions to analyze it.**

b **Compare your answers with a partner.**

4 **Answer these questions about the text on pages 20–21.**

1 What is your reaction? Do you agree or disagree with the main arguments?

2 Does any part make you feel strongly about the topic?

3 Would you like to find different opinions to those presented in the text?

Using the text: selecting information

 When a topic is in the general media or public knowledge, you may already have an opinion about an essay topic you have been given. Lectures, seminars and background reading are also important in creating and focusing your general ideas on a topic. However, it is important when writing academically that you find specific support for any opinion you may have.

Selecting information 1 **Look at these opinions. They are all related to the essay question on page 18. Read the text below and find the information that supports or goes against each opinion.**

1 Strong companies have controlling leaders.

2 A company needs a strong hierarchy.

3 The same leadership style can be used in all situations.

4 Leadership is different in developed countries compared to developing countries.

5 Leadership in manufacturing is different from leadership in office work.

From control to empowerment

Leaders in powerful positions once thought workers should be told what to do and how to do it. They believed strict control was needed for the organization to function efficiently and effectively. Fixed organizational hierarchies, structured jobs and work processes, and detailed procedures let everyone know that those at the top had power and those at the bottom had none.

Today, the old views of the distribution of power are no longer valid. An emphasis on control serves to squelch motivation, innovation and morale rather than produce desired results. Today's leaders share power rather than hoard it. They find ways to increase an organization's brain power by getting everyone involved and committed.

One reason for this is that today's economy is quickly becoming based on information rather than physical assets of land, buildings and machines. Fifty years ago, these assets represented 73 per cent of the assets of non-financial corporations in the United States. By 2002, the proportion was down to around 53 per cent and still declining (IP, 2002). This means that the primary factor of production is human knowledge, which increases the power of employees. The educational and skills level of employees in the United States and other developed countries has also steadily increased over the past several decades. Many people are no longer satisfied working in an organization that doesn't give them opportunity to participate and learn.

When all an organization needed was workers to run machines eight hours a day, traditional command-and-control systems generally worked quite well, but the organization received no benefit from employees' minds. Today, success depends on the intellectual capacity of all employees, and leaders have to face a hard fact: buildings and machines can be owned; people cannot.

2 Compare and discuss the sections you selected in Exercise 1 with a partner.

3 Look again at the opinions in Exercise 1. Do you think the person who wrote them may need change their opinion after reading the text?

Using information **4** Once you have selected a text you may like to use, you need to decide how to use it. Discuss these questions with a partner.

1 The three main ways to use a text in an essay are summarizing, paraphrasing and directly quoting. What do you understand by these terms?

2 When do you think you should use each method? Why?

5 Work with a partner and match each definition (a–c) to its function (1–3).

1 summary
2 paraphrase
3 direct quote

a the exact words of the author that express something in a particular way that mean you do not want to change it

b a shortened version of an original text written in your own words

c a piece that maintains a similar length to the original but is expressed in your own words

6 Look back at the sections you highlighted in Exercise 1 and discuss these questions.

1 Which ideas might you summarize?

2 Which ideas might you paraphrase?

3 Which ideas might you directly quote?

Identifying opinion **7** These are some ways to demonstrate opinion. Underline examples of each in the text on page 24.

1 Change of tense
Example: *Leaders in powerful positions once **thought** workers should be told what to do and how to do it … Today, the old views of the distribution of power **are** no longer valid.*

2 Language of comparison
Example: *An emphasis on control serves to squelch motivation, innovation and morale **rather than** produce desired results.*

3 Use of facts
Example: *Fifty years ago, these assets represented 73 per cent of the assets of non-financial corporations in the United States.*

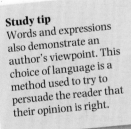

Study tip
Words and expressions also demonstrate an author's viewpoint. This choice of language is a method used to try to persuade the reader that their opinion is right.

8 Match each of the negative verbs (1–4) to its more neutral form (a–d).

1 to sever
2 to squelch
3 to hoard
4 to face a hard fact

a to accept
b to stop
c to cut
d to keep

Language focus 2: dictionary skills – meaning and context

1 **Look at these words taken from this unit and the Academic Word List. How many meanings do you think each word has? Discuss with a partner, then check in a dictionary.**

1 involve   2 energy   3 exhibit   4 issue   5 vision

2 **Look at these sentences and find the correct meaning for each of the words in bold in a dictionary.**

1 These changes will **involve** everybody in the company.

2 The new building's design was **exhibited** in the entrance hall.

3 The next **issue** of the journal is due out next month.

4 The world's **energy** resources are being used rapidly.

5 The tree was blocking my **vision**.

3 **The words in Exercise 1 also appear in the text on pages 20–21. Using the context, find the correct meaning of the words in a dictionary. Are they different to the meanings you found in Exercise 2?**

4 **Choose two words from Exercise 1. Write two sentences for each word to demonstrate different meanings.**

Unit extension

1 **Find another text, one or two pages in length, related to a theory or idea on leadership.**

2 **Quickly skim through the text you have chosen. Write down what you feel is the main idea. Do not worry about detail at this stage.**

3 **Use the questions you created in Exercise 1 on page 23 to produce a more detailed analysis of the text.**

4 **Underline any words you do not understand. Check these words in a dictionary.**

For further practice of the skills covered in this unit, go to www.deltapublishing.co.uk/ resources.

5 **For any words you did not understand that are on the AWL, write a definition and example sentence on vocabulary cards to help you learn their use and meaning.**

3 Language learning

Aims

- Distinguishing between fact and opinion
- Dealing with unknown vocabulary
- Reviewing past and present tense
- Developing summarizing skills
- Understanding common suffixes

Topic focus

1 **Work with a partner and discuss these questions.**

   1 Do you enjoy learning languages?

   2 Do you think you are good at learning languages?

   3 What do you think makes somebody a good language learner?

   4 Do you think some languages are harder to learn than others?

   5 If you could learn a language other than English, which language would you like to learn, and why?

2 **Work with a partner. Which of these is the most difficult skill to master when learning a language? Why?**

   - listening   - reading   - writing   - speaking   - vocabulary   - grammar

3 a **Work with a partner. Which of these factors most and least affects language learning? Rank them in order of importance.**

   - age ☐   - gender ☐   - ability ☐   - motivation ☐

   b **Compare your answer with another pair and discuss your reasons for the order you have chosen.**

Critical thinking: fact and opinion

1 **Work with a partner. Look at these two sentences. Which is a fact, and which is an opinion?**

   a England has a royal family.

   b The royal family should not be allowed to exist any more.

2 **Answer these questions.**

   1 What is the difference between fact and opinion?

   2 Write a definition of fact and a definition of opinion.

   3 How can opinions be made stronger or supported?
      Example: A quote from an expert

3 **Look at the two texts on the next page and do these tasks.**

   1 Match each of these headings to the correct text.
      a The age people learn languages in Europe
      b Is age important in language learning?

   2 Read the texts again; circle the facts and underline the opinions.

   3 Discuss with a partner what helped you to differentiate fact from opinion.

> A valid opinion is one which follows logically from the reason for that opinion. The conclusion is likely to be of more use if there is validity in the opinion.

4 **Look at this essay question and discuss the questions below with a partner.**

> Age has the greatest impact on successful language learning. Discuss.

Study tip
When you select an opinion to use in an essay, you need to think about a number of issues, such as: Where does this opinion come from? Is the person an authority in the area? What evidence is there to support this opinion?

   1 Could you use the opinions from Text A on page 29 in this essay?

   2 Which opinion do you think is the most valid?

   3 Why is this opinion the most valid?

   4 What questions would you need to ask to accept or reject each opinion?

   Examples:
   What factors affect language learning?
   Is age important in language learning?

Finding facts and opinions

5 **Read Text A again and answer these questions.**

   1 Who believes that learning languages from a young age is an advantage?

   2 In what situations does the research support the idea that 'young is best'?

   3 Does Munoz believe that learning a language at home is the same as learning it in the classroom?

   4 Do Singleton and Ryan believe that all the research shows the same outcome?

6 **Read Text B again and answer these questions.**

   1 What has happened to foreign-language learning in Europe between 2003 and 2007?

   2 Which European countries first taught foreign languages from a young age?

   3 When are foreign languages compulsory in the UK?

   4 What do countries that have made the biggest changes have in common?

Text A

During the late 1990s in the UK, a shift in political perceptions of Europe became increasingly more evident. With the appointment of a new prime minister in 1997, strong support for a pro-European political perspective was well reflected in a speech made by Tony Blair at Oxford University. He signalled a belief in the value of early foreign-language learning by claiming that 'Everyone knows that with languages, the earlier you start, the easier they are' (Sharpe, 2001:3).

Blair's claim came as something of a surprise to linguists, applied linguists and educators alike. According to Driscoll and Frost (1999), Singleton and Ryan (2004:227) and Munoz (2006), research does not support this claim. As Munoz (2006:6) elaborates, much of the data on foreign-language learning comes from settings where the child learns in their own home, or from the reportedly immersion contexts in part of Canada, where children have been exposed to two languages across educational, social and public domains (Genesee, 1978/1979). Munoz suggests that the tendency has been for evidence to be over-generalized to the very different context of the classroom, where children experience a substantially more limited exposure. Similarly, Singleton and Ryan's (2004: 116) extensive review of research in this area finds the evidence so far to be inconclusive and at times inconsistent. My personal classroom observations, conducted throughout Europe over a period of some ten years, give me the view that much is achieved in some classrooms through an early start.

Text B

For several decades, Europe has witnessed an increase in the number of years when teaching at least one foreign language is compulsory. Furthermore, there has been a lowering of the age at which this provision begins. These changes have been apparent in a great many countries, especially between 2003 and 2007.

Between 1984 and 2007, around ten countries lowered by at least three years the age at which pupils first had to be taught a foreign language. For example, several countries in southern Europe adopted ambitious policies along these lines. Spain and Italy are now among those countries in which pupils are taught earliest during their education (when aged three and six respectively).

In Luxembourg and Malta, pupils were first taught foreign languages already at a very early stage in 1984. As a result, there was no further change in the age at which this happened until 2007. There was no compulsory curriculum in the United Kingdom (England, Wales and Northern Ireland) until 1988 (England and Wales) and 1989 (Northern Ireland). Under this legislation, languages became a compulsory subject for all pupils from age 11. Initially, this applied up to the age of 16, but later curriculum changes increased flexibility for pupils aged 14 to 16. It is now the case that compulsory language learning starts later (age 11) and ends earlier (age 14) in England, Wales and Northern Ireland than in any other country. Alongside these changes in the secondary curriculum, there have been developments in primary language learning. In England, for example, the Government is committed to making languages a compulsory subject for pupils aged seven to 11 from 2011.

However, this trend towards lowering the age at which children first have to learn languages is far less apparent in several countries of central and eastern Europe. In the great majority of them, children had to begin learning a first foreign language relatively early even in the 1980s. In most cases, that language was Russian. In the Baltic countries, 'Russianization' was especially marked, and the language was taught very early on in compulsory education. However, it was not regarded as a foreign language. Changes in the general organization of education since the beginning of the 1990s may also account for certain variations in some countries.

Between 2003 and 2007, changes occurred in around ten countries. In Belgium (the German-speaking community), the legislation adopted in 2004 made compulsory pre-primary play activities in a foreign language, and language learning from the first year of primary education. Both were features of early education that had been optional but practised in the majority of schools for several decades. Countries in which changes have been greatest are also those in which foreign-language teaching began at a later stage (Bulgaria and Flemish community of Belgium). In Poland, since 2008/09, obligatory foreign-language learning has been introduced for pupils aged seven to ten. From 2008/09 in Portugal, all schools have to offer English to pupils aged six to ten.

Understanding the text: unknown vocabulary

 It is not uncommon when reading an academic text for as much as 20 per cent of the vocabulary to be unfamiliar. Learning the Academic Word List will help reduce this percentage; however, unless detailed knowledge of a text or section of a text is needed, you can often skip words you do not understand.

1 Discuss these questions with a partner.

1 What do you do when you find words in a text you do not understand?

2 What percentage of a text do you need to understand in order to get the general meaning?

2 In this passage, every eighth word is missing. Read it and answer the questions below.

The kind of intelligence which is measured .... IQ tests is a good predictor for ....
in classrooms where the emphasis is on .... about the language (for example, grammar
rules .... vocabulary items). In addition, people who do .... on IQ tests may do well
on .... kinds of tests as well. However, in .... language-learning settings and in
classrooms where .... acquisition through interactive language use is emphasized,
.... has shown that learners with a wide .... of intellectual abilities can be
successful language .... This is especially true if the skills .... are assessed are oral
communication skills rather .... metalinguistic knowledge.

1 Are IQ tests always a good predictor of success in language learning?

2 Is there one type of intelligence that is important in successful language learning?

3 Write a one-sentence summary of the main idea of the paragraph.

3 In this passage, every fifth word is missing. Read it and answer the questions below.

Even people who know .... about the critical period .... are certain that, in
.... programs for second or .... language teaching, 'younger is .... '.
However, both experience and .... show that older learners .... attain high, if not
'................. ', levels of proficiency in .... second language. Furthermore, it ....
essential to think carefully .... the goals of an .... programme and the context
.... which it occurs before .... jump to conclusions about .... necessity – or
even desirability – .... the earliest possible start.

1 Can older learners reach a high level in a language?

2 Should languages be taught from a young age?

3 Write a one-sentence summary of the main idea of the paragraph.

4 Think about the strategies you used to be able to answer the questions in Exercises 2 and 3. Write these down and keep them in mind for future use.

 If you learn to guess the meaning of words from context, or ignore the word completely, you can improve your reading speed. Only use this strategy when detailed understanding is not needed, i.e. only when you are deciding whether texts are relevant to your research questions.

Language focus 1: tense review – past and present simple

1 a **Look at the texts on page 29 and underline the verb forms.**

b **Which tenses are most often used? List the different uses for each example in the text.**

Example: present tense: to talk about thing that happen regularly

2 **Match each of the sentences (1–3) to its corresponding function (a–c).**

1 China produces many products.   **a** present state

2 Age is not important in language learning.   **b** repeated action/habit

3 Lessons start at 9.00 a.m.   **c** general truth

3 **Look at the examples of the present simple in the texts and answer these questions.**

1 Which of the functions from Exercise 2 is most common?

2 Why do you think this is the case?

4 **Past tenses have fewer uses than present tenses and are therefore used less often. How many uses can you think of?**

5 **Look back at the text in Unit 2 (*From control to empowerment* on page 24) and answer these questions.**

1 Which tense is used in each paragraph?

2 Where in the text does the tense change?

3 Why does the tense change?

4 What does this tell you about the structure and organization of this text and the development of the idea?

6 **Complete these sentences by putting the verb in brackets into the correct form. Once you have completed the task, think about why you chose that form.**

1 The results _____ (*show*) that no clear conclusion can be made yet.

2 Strong leaders _____ (*be*) important to a company.

3 The world _____ (*become*) globalized in the 20th century.

4 Britain _____ (*be*) an industrial country.

5 The survey _____ (*find*) that teachers believe learning languages early is beneficial.

6 Water _____ (*boil*) at 100 degrees centigrade.

Using the text: summarizing

 Including summaries as your reference rather than paraphrasing can sometimes be easier. Paraphrasing often requires greater control of grammar and a wider vocabulary range. Summarizing rather than directly quoting in an essay can also be considered better, as it shows your understanding of the topic. However, beware of plagiarism. Plagiarism is when you copy someone else's work and claim it as your own. In most academic cultures, this is not acceptable.

Study tip
One way to avoid plagiarism can be effective note-taking when reading.

1 Work with a partner. Decide whether these statements are true (T) or false (F).

1 Using other people's ideas often strengthens an essay.

2 Borrowing a friend's work and using some of the sentences in your own is fine.

3 Published books are so well written that the ideas cannot be written in another way.

4 A bibliography is enough – you do not need to write a source's details in the text.

2 With a partner, make a list of effective note-taking skills.

Example: Think about your research aims before you start.

3 Use your ideas from Exercise 2 to write a definition of effective notes. Why might effective note-taking help you avoid plagiarism?

4 Look at this essay question and underline the key words. What information might you need to find to answer this question?

Motivation is key to successful language learning. Since girls are more motivated to learn languages, they are more likely to be successful language learners. Discuss.

5 Two students have made notes on a text to help answer the essay question in Exercise 4. Which one is more effective, and why?

Student A

Los que respondieron al cuestionario

dar

Questionnaire respondents were invited to rate their responses as positive, neutral or negative. The first question indicates a fairly positive view among both girls and boys regarding the general importance of being able to speak a foreign language. Moving to the second question, opinions between boys and girls on how positively they felt about learning a foreign language diverged sharply. Boys declared themselves 60% less positive than girls. In particular, no girl was entirely negative about the experience, whilst 11 boys were. (Enever, 2009)

bastante

entre

poder

en cuanto a

marcadamente

mientras que

completamente

Both girls and boys are positive about the importance of being able to speak a foreign language. However, boys' and girls' opinions about how positively they felt about learning a foreign language diverged sharply. Boys are 60% less positive than girls. No girl was entirely negative, but 11 boys were.

Student B

Questionnaire respondents were invited to rate their responses as positive, neutral or negative. The first question indicates a fairly positive view among both girls and boys regarding the general importance of being able to speak a foreign language. Moving to the second question, opinions between boys and girls on how positively they felt about learning a foreign language diverged sharply. Boys declared themselves 60% less positive than girls. In particular, no girl was entirely negative about the experience, whilst 11 boys were. (Enever, 2009)

Relates to part 2 of the question.

Quite a small study – is there other research that supports this?

In this study, boys feel less positive than girls about studying a foreign language.

6 **Using their notes, the two students in Exercise 5 included the summaries below in their essays. Read them and answer these questions.**

1 Which summary is more effective?

2 Which student is more likely to plagiarize?

Student A

According to Enever (2009), boys' and girls' opinions about how positively they felt about learning a foreign language diverged sharply. Boys are 60% less positive than girls.

Student B

Whilst only a small study, Enever (2009) found that, in general, boys were less motivated to learn a foreign language.

7 **Look at Text A on page 29 and answer these questions.**

1 How many words does the author need to summarize the opinion of Driscoll and Frost, Singleton and Ryan, and Munoz?

2 How many words does the author need to summarize the opinion of Singleton and Ryan?

3 What does this tell you about the amount of detail needed in a summary?

8 a **Look at this passage and make notes on it in relation to the essay question in Exercise 4.**

On a number of occasions during the researchers' school visits, however, both teachers and school principals had commented on the quite frequently observed negative response from some boys. Supporting this, when the final report was presented to the School Principals' Steering Committee (a group representing the 44 primary schools), there was much agreement on this finding. Principals from many schools confirmed this tendency amongst the foreign learners of their school also.

b **Summarize the passage in your own words.**

c **Compare your notes and summary with a partner and answer these questions.**

1 Did you identify the same key points?

2 Are your summaries similar?

3 If there are differences between your notes and summaries, can you decide whose is more effective, and why?

Language focus 2: common suffixes

 An affix is added to the beginning or end of a word. There are two forms of affix; suffixes and prefixes. Suffixes are added to the end of a word and in general change the grammar; prefixes are added to the beginning and change the meaning.
Examples: suffix *agree* → *agree***ment**   prefix *agree* → **dis***agree*

1 Look back at the texts in this unit. Find and underline examples of these suffixes.

–ed –ist –or –ence –ion –ier –ive –ory –al –ly

2 a The suffixes in Exercise 1 are widely used. Which make verbs, nouns, adjectives, and adverbs? Work with a partner to complete this table.

verb	noun	adjective	adverb

b Can you think of any other common suffixes? Add them to the table.

3 Complete this table with words from the texts on page 29.

verb	noun	adjective	adverb
	similarity	similar	**1** ....
increase	**2**		
consist	inconsistency	**3**	inconsistently
4	shift		
tend	**5**		

4 Why do you think the words in Exercise 3 were selected? What topic connects them? Can you find any other words in the texts in this unit that can be connected?

Unit extension

1 Find another text connected to this essay question.

Age has the greatest impact on successful language learning. Discuss.

2 Use these steps to analyze the text you have found.

1 Identify the purpose and audience.
2 Scan any contents pages, indexes and subheadings to identify relevant sections.
3 Skim to find out the main ideas.
4 Develop questions to analyze the text.
5 Look critically at any opinions.
6 Select information you could use in the essay.
7 Write a brief summary of the text.

For further practice of the skills covered in this unit, go to www.deltapublishing.co.uk/resources.

4 Sustainability

Topic focus

1 **Look at the title of this unit, then read these sentences and complete the table below with the different forms of the word *sustainability*.**

- The government should do more to promote **sustainable** agriculture.
- The world's use of petrol is **unsustainable**.
- In order to **sustain** this level of population growth, more food needs to be produced.
- There has been **sustained** population growth around the world for hundreds of years.

verb	noun	adjective	adverb
	sustainability		

2 **Write a definition of *sustainable*.**

3 **Work with a partner. Discuss these questions.**

www.CartoonStock.com

  1 Is there anything that concerns you about the future of the world?

  2 Do you think the world has enough food, fuel and other resources for the future?

  3 Do you try to limit the resources you consume?

  4 Should governments try to limit people's consumption?

  5 The world's population has doubled in the last 50 years. How much more do you think it can grow before the world is 'full'?

  6 Is it possible to control population growth?

  7 Who should be responsible for keeping the world's population at a sustainable level?

4 **Look at this essay question. Discuss your opinions with a partner.**

> The world has reached its capacity in terms of the number of people it can support. Unless people dramatically change their behaviour, we are in danger of destroying the world. To what extent do you agree?

Predicting

1 Discuss these questions with a partner.

1 What do you understand by *consumerism*? Check your dictionary if you are not sure.

2 Do you think we live in a society in which consumerism is important?

3 Would it be easy to change people's consumer habits? How might it be possible?

4 Why might change be needed to make a country more sustainable?

5 Whose responsibility is it to make these changes, e.g. the government?

Study tip
Using your knowledge about a topic to make predictions about the content of a text makes it easier to understand. Try to guess the content based on your general knowledge before you start reading.

2 a Look at this book title and and underline the key words.

> *State of the world 2010:*
> *Transforming cultures from consumerism*
> *to sustainability*

b Use your knowledge of this topic to make predictions about the content of the book.

c Discuss your predictions with a partner.

3 a Look at these chapter titles from the book in Exercise 2. Are they topics that you expected to see?

- Traditions old and new
- Education's new assignment: sustainability
- Business and economy: management priorities
- Government's role in design
- Media: broadcasting sustainability
- The power of social movements

b Discuss with a partner what you think each chapter might be about.

4 a Look at the title of the article on pages 37–38, taken from the book in Exercise 2. Write down ideas for how working less might make the world more sustainable.

Example: more free time to walk and cycle rather than drive

b Discuss your ideas with a partner, then read the article to check your ideas.

5 What information could you use from the article when answering the essay question in Exercise 4 on page 35?

6 Answer these questions.

1 How are some people benefiting from being unemployed?

2 With what does the author believe we should swap product consumption?

3 How many worlds would be needed if everyone consumed like America?

4 Why does the author think Americans should consume less?

5 For everyone to keep their job and keep working the same, what needs to happen?

6 Who works more, Americans or Europeans?

7 Who is healthier, Americans or Europeans?

8 Name three benefits of working less.

Reducing work time as a path to sustainability

John de Graaf

There is a positive side to the current recession in the industrial world. Contrary to popular expectations, in some countries – particularly the United States – health outcomes are actually improving. Christopher Ruhm at the University of North Carolina finds a decline in mortality of half a per cent for each one-per-cent increase in US unemployment. How is this happening? Many of the newly jobless suffer from stress, and suicides have increased. But some are using the time off to enable them to improve the rest of their lives – learning to save, be more self-sufficient, finding time to exercise, becoming closer to family and friends.

More important, the crisis has meant a reduction in working hours for most Americans for the first time in decades. Some companies and public agencies have chosen to cut hours rather than making people unemployed. With more time and less money, people are smoking and drinking less, eating fewer restaurant meals, and walking or cycling more. While car sales have fallen dramatically, bicycle sales are increasing. As Americans drive less, they die less often in accidents – US traffic deaths declined by ten per cent from 2007 to 2008. Air pollution from cars and factories is also down, resulting in fewer deaths, especially among children.

In time, workers may find that the increased family time, improved health and other benefits of more leisure outweigh the income losses. This should inspire more efforts to trade productivity for time instead of greater purchasing power.

But we need to do this for another reason: preserving the biosphere for future generations.

The need to limit consumption

Data from the Global Footprint Network suggest that if people in the developing world were to achieve American lifestyles, the world would need four more planets to provide the resources for their products and absorb their wastes. Already – and with half the world's people living in real poverty – the Earth is overpopulated by 40 per cent.

Some environmentalists are anti-cuts and suggest that the world can carry on in the same way by improving technologies and investing in clean energy. Too often, however, technological improvements such as greater fuel efficiency only lead to greater consumption of a product – people drive more, for example.

Industrial countries cannot deny the rights of developing nations to greater economic prosperity while others continue to consume at current levels. That would be asking them to sacrifice so that the rest of the world can consume more awhile longer.

Is there an answer?

The current situation cannot continue, but people in industrial countries are reluctant to reduce their 'standard of living'. Is there a solution to this? Yes: the rich nations of the world must use advances in productivity for free time instead of additional purchasing power. And people must understand that doing so will not be a sacrifice. Rather it will mean substantial improvements in the quality of life.

Technical progress consistently makes production more efficient. For example, hourly labour productivity in rich countries has more than doubled since 1970. The point is simple: to keep everyone employed at the current number of hours while productivity increases, it is necessary to simply produce and consume more. It is unlikely that scientific progress and increases in labour productivity are going to stop. Therefore, in order to limit consumption to current levels (or lower), it will be necessary either to make people unemployed or to reduce everyone's working hours.

Since 1970, the United States has chosen to keep working hours stable – in fact, there is some evidence that US working hours have even increased during the past 40 years.

By contrast, most other industrial countries, especially in Europe, have used shorter workweeks, longer vacations and other strategies to reduce working hours – sometimes significantly. Today, the average American spends 200–300 more hours at work each year than the average European does.

The benefits of shorter hours

Shorter working hours allow more time for connection with friends and family, exercise and healthy eating, citizen and community engagement, attention to hobbies and educational advancement. They also allow appreciation of the natural world, personal emotional and spiritual growth, and conscientious consumer habits. The positive impact of greater free time can be seen by comparing quality-of-life indices for European nations and the United States.

Since 1980, for example, the United States has fallen from eleventh place in life expectancy to fiftieth. West Europeans now live longer than Americans. The United States is now behind Western Europe in virtually every health outcome, despite spending about twice as much per capita for health care. Moreover, Americans, with their more stressful and hurried lives, are nearly twice as likely to suffer from anxiety, depression and other abnormalities of mental health.

Happiness is also affected. While the United States ranks a respectable eleventh in the world in life satisfaction, a recent study found that the four happiest countries in the world – Denmark, the Netherlands, Finland and Sweden – were all characterized by their attentiveness to 'work–life balance'.

The environmental benefits of reduced work time include:

- less need for convenience products. Fast food, for example, is in part a response to an increasingly pressured way of life. Highly packaged and processed foods appeal to those who feel time is short;
- more time to reuse and recycle. Separating wastes into paper, plastics, metals, compost or rubbish takes time;
- time to make other behavioural choices, such as drying one's clothes on a clothesline rather than in a dryer;
- time to choose slower and more energy-friendly forms of transport, including walking, cycling or public transport rather than driving;
- time to make careful consumer choices, including for certified products like Fair Trade and organic products, or local rather than international products.

Moreover, reductions in work time translate rapidly into reductions in energy use, carbon footprints and pollution. A study conducted by the Center for Economic and Policy Research concluded that if Americans were to reduce their working hours to European levels, they would almost automatically reduce their energy/carbon impacts by 20–30 per cent.

Re-visioning the future

Clearly the world is at a crossroads. For all the benefits that investments in 'green jobs' and new energy technologies will surely provide, they are only part of what's needed for long-run sustainability. To survive and to let people in developing countries somehow achieve secure and modest comfort, material economic growth in rich nations simply must be limited. Yet this must be done without stopping the progress of science and the advance of productivity and without making millions unemployed. Ultimately, it can only be done by trading gains in productivity for time, by reducing the hours of labour and sharing them equitably. All of this means limiting greed, understanding that a life less rich materially but more rich temporally is not self-sacrifice.

Language focus 1: prefixes

Word formation **1 A prefix is an affix which changes the meaning of a word (see Unit 3).**

advantage → **dis**advantage

employed → **un**employed

developed → **under**developed

Underline the prefixes used in the text on pages 37–38.

Prefix meanings **2 Match these prefixes (1–8) to their meaning (a–h). Use the context of the text on pages 37–38 to help you.**

1 un–	a to do again
2 re–	b between
3 en–	c to put someone or something in a particular state or have a particular quality
4 anti–	
5 micro–	d together with
6 self–	e against
7 co–	f very small
8 inter–	g to show a negative or opposite
	h alone

3 Work with a partner. How many words can you think of using each prefix in Exercise 2?

Examples: self-sufficient, self-aware, self-serving

4 From the words you wrote in Exercise 3, choose one word for each prefix and write an example sentence using each of them.

Language activation **5 Complete these sentences using the prefixes from Exercise 2 and the words in brackets. Change the grammatical form of the words if necessary.**

1 The ___interaction___ (*action*) between a manager and their staff can vary culturally.

2 The company operates in an _____ (*national*) market.

3 The image was _____ (*large*) so that it could be studied in detail.

4 Left-wing politics can be considered _____ (*capitalist*).

5 A section of the form was incomplete and it had to be _____ (*submit*).

6 The value of an employee was considered _____ (*important*) in the past compared to the value of buildings and machinery.

7 _____ (*electronics*) have developed significantly in terms of both their power and the size of each component.

8 An individual's writing skills can be enhanced by through _____ (*assessment*) prior to submitting the work for approval or marking.

9 Many academic texts are _____ (*authored*) to bring together a wider range academic skills.

10 He was _____ (*aware*) of the change in time, so he was late for the meeting.

Critical thinking: reasons and conclusions

 The reason is the basis on which an argument is made. It is the foundation for the conclusion that is drawn. This can sometimes be thought of as a cause-and-effect relationship.

Argument structure 1 **Read these sentences, then underline the reasons and circle the conclusions.**

1 Consuming becomes a habit for people because they do not take the time to think and make choices based on their own best interests.

2 After a certain point, money does not make people happier. Yes, people need a certain level of money, but the lust for more causes people to ignore the important things like friends, family and community.

3 People in America consume more and are therefore happier.

4 As more people drive, then more people will become fat.

5 Using energy-friendly transport such as cycling would reduce people's energy consumption.

Argument analysis

 It is important to analyze the logic of an argument. Conclusions need to be linked logically to a reason to give an argument strength.
For example, we can analyze sentence 3 of Exercise 1 as follows:
- Does consumption make people happy? – Possibly
- Are there other things that could be making Americans happy? – Yes
- Does consumption make people have other feelings? – Yes (e.g. guilt)

2 **Analyze sentences 4 and 5 in Exercise 1 in the same way, thinking about the logic in the connection between reason and conclusion.**

3 **Discuss these questions with a partner.**

1 Which argument in Exercise 1 do you think is the most logical?

2 What makes it the most logical?

3 How can you evaluate the strength of an argument?

4 **Look at these criteria for evaluating the logic of an argument. Can you add any more?**

1 Is there a logical correlation between the reason and conclusion?

2 Is there a logical cause-and-effect relationship between the reason and the conclusion?

3 Is there an unwritten assumption the author needs to make for the conclusion to make sense?

 A logical argument is not always a strong argument. Other factors that have influenced the outcome, such as the strength of the evidence, need to be considered.

5 **Look at these arguments. Use the criteria you established in Exercise 4 to evaluate each one.**

1 Improving technology and clean energy will reduce people's levels of consumption.

2 Forcing people to consume less will lead to greater sustainability.

3 Providing consumers with alternative, more sustainable energy supplies does not necessarily mean these will be used by consumers.

Using the text: paraphrasing

Introduction to paraphrasing

1 Discuss these questions with a partner.

1 What is paraphrasing?

2 When would you paraphrase?

3 Why do we paraphrase?

4 How can you effectively paraphrase?

> **Study tip**
> Paraphrasing often involves changing vocabulary for a synonym (a word with a similar meaning), changing word order and changing word formation. Synonyms with exactly the same meaning can be hard to select. Where possible, try not to translate word for word, but create a new sentence using vocabulary you already know.

2 A paraphrase needs to be different in terms of the language but keep the same meaning as the original text. Read this sentence and decide which of the paraphrases below (a–c) is the best.

Although the idea seems pessimistic and is little discussed, it is possible that world population – at 6.8 billion people today and growing by 216,000 a day – has already surpassed sustainable levels, even if everyone on Earth achieved merely modest European rather than lavish North American consumption levels.

a The world's population at 6.8 billion people has already gone beyond sustainable levels. That is despite the fact that everyone has achieved modest European consumption levels and is not as high as American consumption levels. The continued increase of 216,000 people per day cannot be sustained.

b Although the idea seems negative and is rarely discussed, it is possible that world population – at 6.8 billion people today and increasing by 216,000 per day – has already gone beyond sustainable levels, even if everyone on Earth reached the lower European rather than the extravagant North American consumption levels.

c The world's population currently stands at 6.8 billion people and continues to increase by 216,000 per day. Although this thought may seem negative and rarely discussed, it could be argued that world population has gone beyond sustainable levels, even if everyone were to consume at lower rate such as European consumption levels rather than North American levels.

Paraphrasing practice

3 Changing vocabulary is one method of paraphrasing. Look at these words. Use your own knowledge or a dictionary to think of a synonymous word or phrase.

1 idea *thought*

2 pessimistic

3 possible

4 growing

5 level

6 achieved

7 consume

8 everyone

4 Re-ordering sentences or parts of sentences is another technique to use in paraphrasing. It often requires words to be added, removed or changed. Look at these sentences and underline the part(s) of each one that could be put in a different position.

1 As people consume more convenience foods, it results in health and weight issues.

2 For the world to truly become sustainable, population growth needs to be limited.

3 American consumption levels are amongst the highest in the world, and are even four times higher than Western European consumption levels.

4 Increasing people's knowledge of local products and services could help reduce the impact of transporting goods around the world.

5 Changing word formation is another technique used in paraphrasing. It also often requires words to be added, removed or changed. Rewrite each of these sentences, changing the word in bold to the part of speech indicated in brackets.

1 The **modification** of habits is required to maintain sustainability. (*adjective*)
Modified habits are required to maintain sustainability.

2 The **possibility** of environmental disaster is high. (*adjective*)

3 The **growing** population of certain countries is causing much environmental damage. (*noun*)

4 The government **achieved** its target of reduced energy consumption. (*noun*)

6 Paraphrase these sentences using the three techniques from Exercises 3–5.

1 A greater emphasis needs to be placed on work–life balance.

2 Education is a key method for changing people's habits.

3 Governments need to take responsibility for changing people's lifestyle.

7 a Look at the text below and find sentences that support each of these opinions.

1 Higher tax is one method of changing people's behaviour.

2 Greater choice is needed to change people's behaviour.

b Paraphrase the sentences you have selected using techniques taught in this unit.

> **Study tip**
> Paraphrasing can be more challenging in terms of your use of English. If you are not confident using the techniques in this section, use the summarizing methods taught in the previous unit.

Choice editors remove environmentally offensive products from commercial consideration, for example smog-producing charcoal lighter fluid in Los Angeles or leaded gasoline in Europe and North America. Or they make such products expensive to use, like Ireland's tax of plastic shopping bags, which has reduced plastic-bag use by 90 per cent. But like any good editor, choice editors cannot just chop. They must offer options or, at the very least – in the words of environmental reporter Leo Hickman – a sufficiently compelling illusion of choice. In Los Angeles, backyard cooks denied their lighter fluid had the choice of chimney or electric briquette fire starters. In Ireland, shoppers can purchase any number of cloth bags, some trendy or stylish. And in Australia and a growing number of countries consumers are encouraged to buy more energy-efficient light bulbs and other innovative methods of lighting.

Language focus 2: dictionary skills – word form

1 Look at this dictionary entry. What additional information, other than the meaning of *consumption*, can you find?

This indicates that the word is a noun.

This indicates that the word is an uncountable noun.

This shows the most common use.

consumption /kən'sʌmpʃən/ *n.* (U)
1 **AMOUNT OF STH USED** ➤ the amount of oil, energy, electricity, etc. that is used ➤ **energy/fuel consumption**: *dramatic rises in fuel consumption, Vigorous exercise increases oxygen consumption.*
2 **EATING/DRINKING a)** *formal* the act of eating or drinking ➤ **consume [+ of]** *The consumption of alcohol on the premises is forbidden.* **fit/unfit for human consumption** = safe/not safe to eat: *The meat was declared unfit for human consumption.* **b)** the amount of a substance that people eat, drink, smoke, etc. **caffeine/tobacco/alcohol consumption** *The government wants to reduce tobacco consumption by 40%.*
3 **BUYING** the act of buying and using products; ➤ **consume, consumer**; *art intended for* **mass consumption** = to be seen by lots of people. *China's austerity programme has cut* **domestic consumption** = products bought in the country they were produced. **conspicuous consumption** = when people buy expensive products to prove they are rich

These show common collocations.

2 Whilst definition 1 in the above entry may be the most common use, you may encounter the other uses more frequently when studying different subjects. In which subject might each meaning be the most common?

3 Look in your dictionary. What other information does it contain about a word?

Unit extension

1 Look at the essay question on page 35 (Exercise 4). Search for topics related to this question, such as *sustainability*, *population growth*, etc., on the Internet. Find an article that expresses opinions on this topic.

2 Highlight the reasons and conclusions in the text you have selected.

3 Choose two of the reasons/conclusions you highlighted in Exercise 2 that you could use when answering the essay question. Paraphrase them using the techniques studied in this unit.

For further practice of the skills covered in this unit, go to www.deltapublishing.co.uk/resources.

5 Crime

- Identifying relationships between ideas and theories
- Modals and hedging language
- Identifying cause and connection
- Discussing texts in seminars
- Alternative and counter-arguments

Topic focus

1 Look at the three people above and discuss these questions.

  1 Which person do you think is most likely to commit a crime?

  2 Why did you select this person?

  3 Do you think it is possible to identify a criminal by their physical appearance?

  4 How can you identify someone who is likely to commit a crime?

2 Look at these opinions on crime. Which one(s) do you think are true?

1 You can identify a criminal by their physical features.

2 Labelling somebody a 'criminal' will make them commit more crime.

3 All people are criminals to a certain extent, but society controls this behaviour.

3 a These are key words in a text. Use a dictionary to find their meanings. What is the grammatical form of each word?

  1 genetic   2 predetermined   3 physique   4 hereditary   5 body-type

b Now you know these are key words, what do you think the topic of the text will be?

1 In earlier units, we have looked at how to identify whether a text was important to read. How do you identify the importance of an idea within a text?

2 Look at the text below and answer these questions.

   1 How many body types did Sheldon identify?

   2 Whose original work informed Sheldon's work?

   3 Which body type did Sheldon identify as the one most likely to commit crime?

   4 Is Sheldon's theory considered to be true today?

   5 What is the main idea in the text?

Biological and genetic explanations of crime

Cesare Lombroso's work on the 'born criminal' identified the primitive, basic differences that he believed were the direct cause of crime. Lombroso was not alone in his views on the biological basis of crime. A contemporary, Raffaele Garofalo (1852–1934), shared the belief that certain physical characteristics indicate a criminal nature. Enrico Ferri (1856–1929) added a social dimension to Lombroso's work and argued that criminals should not be held personally or morally responsible for their actions because forces outside their control caused criminality.

Advocates of the **inheritance school**, such as Henry Goddard, Richard Dugdale and Arthur Estabrook, traced several generations of crime-prone families, finding evidence that criminal tendencies were based on genetics. Their conclusion: traits deemed socially inferior could be passed down generation to generation through inheritance. Modern scholars point out that these families lived in severe poverty, so that social rather than biological factors may have been at the root of their problems.

The body-build, or **somatotype**, school, developed more than 50 years ago by William Sheldon, held that criminals have distinct physiques that make them susceptible to particular types of antisocial behaviour. Three types of body build were identified:

- **Mesomorphs** have well-developed muscles and an athletic appearance. They are active, aggressive, sometimes violent and the most likely to be criminals.
- **Endomorphs** have heavy builds and are slow moving. They are known for lethargic behaviour, meaning that they are less likely to commit violent crime and more willing to engage in less strenuous criminal activities.
- **Ectomorphs** are tall and thin, and less social and more intellectual than the other types.

The work of Lombroso and his contemporaries is regarded today as a historical curiosity, not scientific fact. Their research methodology has been discredited because they did not use control groups from the general population to compare results. Many of the traits they assumed to be inherited are not really genetically determined but could be caused by deprivation in surroundings and diet. Even if most criminals shared some biological traits, they might be products not of heredity but of some environmental condition, such as poor nutrition or healthcare. Unusual appearance, and not behaviour, may have prompted people to be labelled and punished by the justice system. In his later writings, even Lombroso admitted that the born criminal was just one of many types.

3 a Complete the text below with the words/phrases in the box.

apply	connected	considered	develop
	starting point	understanding	

Assessing the importance of ideas

An idea does not have to be true to be **1** _____ important in a field. Sheldon's ideas on why people commit a crime are largely considered to not be true; however, his work gave an important **2** _____ for further research. His ideas helped the field of criminology to **3** _____ , and for further research to develop our understanding of the issues. Arguably, many theories can also be considered to not **4** _____ to the real world and so are not true in this sense; however, these theories provide a basis for **5** _____ and evaluating a situation. When presented with a range of ideas on a related topic, it is important to see how they are **6** _____ and the status which a theory has within its field.

b Discuss these questions with a partner.

1 Are biological explanations of crime likely to be true?
2 Are biological explanations of crime considered important?

4 Look at the text on page 47 and answer these questions.

1 The words *deviance* and *deviant* appear throughout the text. Use the context to try to define the meaning of these words.
2 Who is responsible for creating the most labels?
3 What is the difference between a rich child stealing an apple and a poor child stealing an apple?
4 Is all crime punished?
5 How does labelling affect a person's view of themselves?
6 What is the main criticism of labelling theory?
7 What alternative cause of criminal behaviour does the text present?

5 Discuss these questions with a partner.

1 How are these different ideas in the two texts (pages 45 and 47) connected?
   a the work of Lombroso   **b** body-type studies   **c** inheritance school   **d** labelling
2 Could any of these theories be dismissed today as a cause for crime?
3 If a theory can be dismissed as a cause, why might it still be considered important?
4 Are any of these theories strong enough to be considered the sole or main cause of crime?
5 Much modern research focuses on studying twins. Why do you think this might be the case?
6 Are these two texts enough to form a strong opinion about these ideas for use in an essay?

Sociological theories of crime

One of the most important approaches to the understanding of criminality is called 'labelling theory'. Labelling theorists interpret deviance not as a set of characteristics of individuals or groups, but as the process of interaction between deviants and non-deviants. In their view, we must discover why some people come to be given a 'deviant' label in order to understand the nature of the deviance itself.

People who represent the forces of law and order, or are able to impose definitions on others, do most of the labelling. The labels that create categories of deviance thus express the power structure of society. By and large, the rules in terms of which deviance is defined are framed by the wealthy for the poor, by men for women, by older people for younger people, and by ethnic majorities for minority groups. For example, many children go into other people's gardens, steal fruit or miss school. In a rich neighbourhood, these might be regarded by parents, teachers and police alike as innocent pastimes of childhood. In poor areas, they might be seen as evidence of possible causes of young people becoming criminalized. Once a child is labelled a criminal, he or she is likely to be considered untrustworthy by teachers and prospective employers. In both instances, the acts are the same, but they are given different meanings.

Labelling not only affects how others see an individual, but also influences the individual's sense of self. Edwin Lemert (1972) put forward a model for understanding how deviance can either exist with or become central to a person's identity. Lemert argued that deviance is actually quite commonplace, and people usually get away with it. For example, traffic offences are rarely punished, while others, such as small-scale theft from the workplace, are often 'overlooked'. In most cases, these acts do not become a main part of self-identity – these acts become acceptable and normal. In some cases, however, the person is labelled as a criminal or delinquent, and individuals come to accept the label and see themselves as deviant. In such instances, the label can become central to a person's identity and lead to a continuation or intensification of the deviant behaviour.

Critics of labelling theory argue that labelling theorists neglect the process that leads to acts defined as deviant. Labelling certain acts as deviant is not completely arbitrary; differences in socialization, attitudes and opportunities influence how far people engage in behaviour likely to be labelled deviant. It is not the labelling that leads to stealing in the first place so much as the background they come from. It is also not clear whether labelling actually does have the effect of increasing deviant conduct. Delinquent behaviour tends to increase following conviction, but is this the result of the labelling itself? Other factors such as increased interaction with other delinquents or learning new criminal opportunities may be involved.

6 Match each theory (1–3) to an explanation of its importance (a–c).

1 the work of Lombroso

2 body-type studies

3 labelling

a These studies, whilst well known, have been shown to have little or no connection with the causes of crime.

b This work was important, as it formed some of the early basis for studying biological causes of crime.

c This theory is an important environmental study of the causes of crime, but so far has not been proven to be true.

Language focus 1: modals and hedging

> Often ideas are not proven or disproven 100%. It is therefore common in academic writing to use cautious language to present an idea. Even when you strongly disagree with a point, it is still common to 'hedge' your opinion with the language you use.

1 **Find these words and phrases in the text on page 47. What is the function of each, and what idea do they relate to?**

1 might be regarded *a possible way of thinking – about children's behaviour*

2 might be seen

3 likely to be considered

4 argued that

5 rarely

6 often

7 In most cases

8 In some cases

9 can become

10 likely

11 It is also not clear

12 tends to

13 may be involved

2 a **Look at this paragraph. The ideas here are less cautious than they are in the original. What weakness does this create?**

A child stealing fruit will be considered to simply be having fun, whilst a child stealing fruit in a poor neighbourhood will be labelled a thief. This label will make the child change their view of themselves and result in them defining themselves as a criminal. This label is going to lead to the child continuing in a life of crime and make the individual commit even more offences. Therefore it is clear that the labelling of the act leads to an increase in crime.

b **Rewrite the paragraph using expressions from Exercise 1 to make it more cautious.**

3 **Look again at the text on page 45 and answer these questions.**

1 Underline the cautious language used.

2 What does this tell you about the text?

3 Which idea do you think has largely been disproved, and which is still more open to debate?

4 How can identifying this language help you see the importance of an idea?

4 **Look at these sentences. Do they need to be more assertive, less assertive or are they neutral?**

1 Physical characteristics perhaps do not provide strong evidence for the understanding of criminal behaviour.

2 Labelling leads to criminal behaviour.

3 Twin studies may provide some insight into the role of genetics and environment.

5 **Using cautious language, write a brief summary of each theory listed in Exercise 6 on page 47. Cover these topics:**

● Importance in the field

● Strength(s) of the theory

● Weakness(es) in the theory

Critical thinking: cause and connection

Study tip
It is important to think about the causes of and connections between issues. Ask yourself questions such as *Could this be the cause? Is there a relationship between X and Y? How strong is the relationship?*

1 a **Look at this paragraph from a student's essay. Think back to the text you read on page 45 and underline the parts of the original text that have been misrepresented.**

   b **How has the student misrepresented the ideas from the text?**

Biology and genetics play a major role in the root causes of crime. According to Siegel (2010), it can be stated that traits deemed socially inferior could be passed down generation to generation through inheritance. Additionally, research has shown that there are differences in physique between criminal and non-criminal males. Thus it can be argued that criminals are born, not created by society.

2 **Look back at the text on page 45 and answer these questions.**

   1 Which parts of the text present possible connections between biology and crime?

   2 Which parts of the text dismiss these connections?

   3 What, as well as biology, contributes towards criminality?

3 **Look at these statements about the connection between biology/genetics and crime. According to the text, which statement has the greatest truth?**

   a Biological causes of crime have been completely dismissed.

   b Biological causes of crime are widely accepted.

   c Biological causes of crime are only accepted in relation to other causes.

4 **Look at the text on page 47 and answer these questions.**

   1 Which paragraphs present possible connections between labelling and crime?

   2 Which paragraphs dismiss these connections?

5 **Work in pairs.**

   Student A: Look at the text on page 45.   Student B: Look at the text on page 47.

   a **Underline language that shows 1) how ideas are connected to crime; 2) criticism of a cause; and 3) origins or connections between causes.**

   Examples:

   Cesare Lombroso's work on the 'born criminal' <u>identified</u> the primitive, basic differences that he believed were the <u>direct cause of</u> crime. (connection)

   Modern scholars <u>point out that</u> these families lived in severe poverty, so that social <u>rather than</u> biological factors may have been <u>at the root of</u> their <u>problems.</u> (criticism)

   b **Record the phrases you have underlined in this table.**

connecting theories	criticizing theories	praising theories
identified direct cause of	point out that rather than at the root of [...] problem(s)	

6 **Discuss these questions with a partner.**

   1 Which idea (biology or labelling) is dismissed the most strongly?

   2 What language helped you to make this decision?

Using the text: discussing texts

1 **Look back at the text on page 45 and discuss these questions with a partner.**

 1 What is the main idea of the text?

 2 What is your opinion of the ideas in the text?

 3 Would you feel comfortable discussing this text in a seminar? Why? / Why not?

2 a **Think about presenting the text on page 45 in a seminar. What would you need to focus on in the text?**

 b **Read the text again. In each paragraph:**

 ● find the main idea;

 ● find the supporting idea;

 ● say how the main idea is supported, e.g. example, explanation, quote;

 ● note your personal reaction to it.

3 **Compare your answers to Exercise 2 with a partner. Have you selected the same main and supporting ideas? Have you both reacted in the same way to the texts?**

4 **Repeat Exercises 2 and 3 for the text on page 47.**

5 a **Respond to the questions in this survey.**

On a scale of 1 to 10, how would you feel about doing each of the following in a seminar?

Discussing your reactions to the text

Easy									Difficult
1	2	3	4	5	6	7	8	9	10

Discussing the significance of this idea in the field of criminology

Easy									Difficult
1	2	3	4	5	6	7	8	9	10

Presenting this text in class (summarizing the main ideas and your reaction to others)

Easy									Difficult
1	2	3	4	5	6	7	8	9	10

 b **Compare and discuss your responses with a partner.**

6 **Answer these questions with a partner.**

 1 What are the features of a good presentation? Example: well researched

 2 What differences would there be between a normal presentation and discussing and presenting a text?

7 a **Work in groups of four (Students A–D). Use the information from this section.**

 Student A: Present the first text (page 45).

 Student B: Present the second text (page 47).

 Students C and D: Listen to the presentations and evaluate these points:
 ● Were all main points covered?
 ● Did the student have to refer to the text a lot?
 ● Did they have a clear reaction to the topic?

 b **As a group, discuss and compare the ideas of both texts.**

Language focus 2: alternative and counter-arguments

1 One of the most common words for countering an argument is *however*.
Working with a partner, what synonyms of *however* can you think of?
Use the texts in this unit to help you.

2 Look at these words. Which words are used to support an argument, and which are used to counter one?

- in addition   • furthermore   • however   • on the other hand   • moreover
- nonetheless   • not only … but also   • at the same time   • even though
- neither … nor   • argue that

3 Complete these sentences using the words and phrases in Exercise 2.

1 Delinquent behaviour tends to increase following conviction; _____ , is this the result of the labelling itself?

2 Labelling _____ affects how others see an individual _____ influences the individual's sense of self.

3 Critics of labelling theory _____ labelling theorists neglect the process that leads to acts defined as deviant.

4 In some cases, _____ , normalization does not occur, and the person is labelled as a criminal or delinquent.

4 Use some of the other words and phrases from Exercise 2 to create at least three sentences of your own related to the theme of crime.

Unit extension

1 Conduct further research into the causes of crime. Try to find one other theory regarding these causes.

2 Choose an idea you have found that is not the same as one of those in the book. Prepare to summarize it and react to the ideas for a small-group discussion.

3 Is one idea on the causes of crime given more importance than others? Has this theory helped to develop any other theories related to crime?

For further practice of the skills covered in this unit, go to www.deltapublishing.co.uk/resources.

6 Revision

Understanding the text

Predicting content (Unit 4)

1 a Look at the title of the text on the next page and the words in bold. What do you think this text will be about?

  b Compare your answer with a partner.

Skimming (Unit 2)

2 a Work with a partner to write a definition of skimming and its purpose.

  b Compare your definition with another pair.

3 Read the text on the next page and answer these questions.
  1 What subject did Hofstede study?
  2 Which company did he study?
  3 How many factors related to his main subject did he study?

Scanning (Unit 2)

4 a Work with a partner to write a definition of scanning and its purpose.

  b Compare your answer with another pair.

5 Match each of these headings (a–e) to a section of the text on the next page (1–5).
  a A view on time and culture
  b Cultures with typically male or female behaviour
  c How control is viewed in different cultures
  d The importance of rules in different cultures
  e The importance of group or personal responsibility

Dealing with unknown vocabulary

6 a Underline the words you do not know in the text on the next page.

  b Discuss these questions with a partner.
   1 How much of the text do you think you understood?
   2 Which words did you not understand?
   3 Which words do you think you need to check the meaning of?

Purpose and audience (Unit 1)

7 a Look again at the text and choose its correct function (a, b or c).
  a to persuade   b to inform   c to argue

  b Highlight language that helped you make this decision.

Hofstede's comparison of national cultures

Geert Hofstede is a Dutch academic who has conducted widely quoted studies of national cultural differences. The second edition of his research (Hofstede, 2001) extends and refines the conclusions of his original work, which was based on a survey of the attitudes of 116,000 IBM employees, one of the earliest global companies. The research inspired many empirical studies with non-IBM employees in both the original countries in which IBM operated and in places where they did not. Kirkman et al. (2006) reviewed many of these and concluded that 'most of the country differences predicted by Hofstede were supported' (p.308).

Hofstede (2001) defined culture as a collective programming of people's minds, which influences how they react to events in the workplace. He identified five dimensions of culture and sought to measure how people in different countries vary in their attitudes to them.

1 **Power distance** (PD) is 'the extent to which the less powerful members of ... organizations within a country expect and accept that power is distributed unevenly' (Hofstede and Hofstede, 2005, p.46). One of the ways in which countries differ is in how power and authority are distributed. Related to this is how the people view the resultant inequality. In some, the existence of inequality in boss–subordinate relationships is seen as undesirable, while in others people see it as part of the natural order of things. The questionnaire allowed the researchers to calculate scores for PD, countries with a high PD being those where people accepted inequality. Those with high scores included Malaysia, Mexico, Venezuela, Arab countries, China, France and Brazil. Those with low PD scores included Australia, Germany, Great Britain, Sweden and Norway.

2 **Uncertainty avoidance** is 'the extent to which members of a culture feel threatened by ambiguous or unknown situations' (Hofstede and Hofstede, 2005, p.167). People in some cultures tolerate ambiguity and uncertainty quite readily – if things are not clear, they will improvise or use their initiative. Others are reluctant to move without clear rules or instructions. High scores, indicating low intolerance of uncertainty, were obtained in Latin American, Latin European and Mediterranean countries, and for Japan and Korea. Low scores were recorded in Asian countries other than Japan and Korea and in the United States, Great Britain, Sweden and Denmark.

3 Hofstede and Hofstede (2005) distinguish between **individualism and collectivism:** 'Individualism pertains to societies in which the ties between individuals are loose: everyone is expected to look after himself or herself and his or her immediate family. Collectivism, as its opposite, pertains to societies in which people, from birth onwards, are integrating into strong, cohesive in-groups which, throughout people's lifetime, continue to protect them in exchange for unquestioning loyalty.' (p.76)

Some people live in societies in which the power of the group prevails: there is an emphasis on collective action and mutual responsibility, and on helping each other through difficulties. Other societies emphasize the individual, and his or her responsibility for their position in life. High scores on the individualism dimension occurred in wealthy countries such as the United States, Australia, Great Britain and Canada. Low scores occurred in poor countries such as the less-developed South American and Asian countries.

4 **Masculinity and femininity.** 'A society is called masculine when emotional gender roles are clearly distinct: men are supposed to be assertive, tough and focused on material success, whereas women are supposed to be modest, tender and concerned with the quality of life. A society is called feminine when emotional gender roles overlap (i.e. both men and women are supposed to be modest, tender and concerned with the quality of life).' (Hofstede and Hofstede, 2005, p.120)

The research showed that societies differ in the desirability of assertive behaviour (labelled masculinity) and of modest behaviour (femininity). Many societies expect men to seek achievements outside the home, while women care for things within the home. Masculinity scores were not related to economic wealth. The most feminine countries were Sweden, Norway, the Netherlands and Denmark. Masculine countries include Japan, Austria, Germany, China and the United States.

5 **Long-term and short-term orientation.** Long-term orientation stands for encouraging virtues linked to future rewards such as saving and perseverance. Short-term orientation places greater emphasis on the past and present, in particular tradition and fulfilling social obligations (Hofstede and Hofstede, 2005). Countries with high LTO scores include China, Hong Kong, Taiwan and Japan. Great Britain, Australia, New Zealand, the United States and Canada have a short-term orientation, in which many people see spending not saving as a virtue.

Critical thinking

Questions to analyze texts (Unit 2)

1 a Look at these topics and think of questions related to them that you could write to analyze the text on page 53.

Example: What is Hofstede's main argument? What evidence is presented to support this? How strong is the evidence?

- main point
- supporting idea
- argument
- evidence
- assumption
- bias
- facts
- opinions
- organization
- definitions

b Compare your questions with a partner.

c Look back at the text and answer your questions.

2 Think in particular about facts, opinions, arguments and evidence you found when answering your questions in Exercise 1. What criticisms could you make of Hofstede's work?

Identifying viewpoint (Unit 1)

3 a Look at your answers to the questions you wrote in Exercise 1. How do your opinions and views compare to these ideas?

> **Limitations of Hofstede's work**
>
> Other scholars have drawn attention to some limitation of Hofstede's work, including;
>
> - the small (and so possibly unrepresentative) number of respondents in some countries;
> - reducing a phenomenon as complex as a nation's culture to five dimensions;
> - basing the original sample on employees of a single multinational;
> - the possibility that cultures change over time;
> - the variety of cultures within a country (e.g. between religious or ethnic groups);
> - the likelihood of differences of cultures within IBM. (McSweeny, 2002)

b If any of the criticisms above are different to yours, do you agree with them? Why? / Why not?

Distinguishing fact from opinion (Unit 3)

4 Look at these statements based on the text on page 53. Which are facts and which are opinions? What evidence would need to be found to support each opinion?

1 116,000 people were surveyed.

2 The survey was based on only one company.

3 It is not realistic to reduce a country's culture to only five dimensions.

4 Cultures possibly change over time.

5 The questionnaire showed that people in Great Britain do not accept inequality.

6 There could be different cultures within a country.

5 In each of these sentences, underline the reason and circle the conclusion.

1 The small (and so possibly unrepresentative) number of respondents in some countries means that conclusions have been made about countries that may not be true for the larger population.

2 Culture is a difficult concept to define; therefore, reducing a phenomenon as complex as a nation's culture to five dimensions oversimplifies the topic.

3 Culture does not simply relate to country. A family, organization, religion or ethnic group can have their own culture. Hofstede's work is limited, then, in that it is based only on employees of a single multinational.

Cause and connection (Unit 5)

6 Read this case study and answer the questions below.

A French manager starts work in a British company and expects his employees to follow his instructions and orders precisely. Whilst he is away on a business trip, a number of things go wrong with a project his team are working on. His team decide, rather than to bother him, that they will use their own initiative and take responsibility for any decisions they make. On his return to work, the manager discovers that the project has been completed, but not in exactly the way he expected. In a following meeting, he raises these issues, and an argument follows. The British staff cannot believe they are being criticized for using their own initiative and feel they are being spoken to like children. The French manager feels they have been disrespectful of his authority and that his orders were not followed clearly.

www.CartoonStock.com

1 Why do you think the confusion occurred between the French manager and his British employees?

2 How is culture connected to the issue?

3 According to Hofstede's theory, what was the cause of the problem?

Using the text

Selecting the text (Unit 1) **1 Look at the two essay questions below and discuss these questions with a partner.**

1 Which one would the text on page 53 be most useful for?

2 How might it be useful?

a

> Intercultural communication difficulties can be one of the main causes for a business failing in a new market. To what extent do you agree?

b

> Define different ways in which organizations and individuals behave in different cultures.

Selecting information (Unit 2) **2 Look at these opinions and select the part of the text from page 53 that would best support each one. Compare your answers with a partner.**

1 The equality between managers and their employees depends very much on the cultural norm.

2 In certain cultures, clear rules are integral to the effective running and operation of a business.

3 The extent to which a country values traditions varies throughout the world.

Summarizing (Unit 3) **3 This is an example note for paragraph 1 and an accompanying summary.**

> Hofstede – 116,000 IBM employees – many countries – 5 cultural differences
> Hofstede (2001) analyzed 116,000 IBM employees in different countries and identified five main cultural differences.

Take notes for each following section of the text on page 53 and write a short summary (one or two sentences) for each one.

Paraphrasing (Unit 4) **4 a Paraphrase these parts of the text from page 53.**

1 Hofstede (2001) defined culture as a collective programming of people's minds, which influences how they react to events in the workplace.
   According to Hofstede (2001), culture is the common learned behaviours that impact on behaviour within the workplace.

2 People in some cultures tolerate ambiguity and uncertainty quite readily – if things are not clear, they will improvise or use their initiative.

3 The research showed that societies differ in the desirability of assertive behaviour (labelled masculinity) and of modest behaviour (femininity).

4 'Long-term orientation' stands for encouraging virtues linked to future rewards such as saving and perseverance.

b Compare your paraphrases with a partner. Check that they are sufficiently different from the original, but keep the same meaning.

Discussing texts in seminars (Unit 5) **5 Use your notes from Exercise 3 to produce a complete summary of the text, as follows.**

1 Join your paragraph summaries together to produce a single text summary.

2 Think about your opinion and reaction to Hofstede's ideas.

3 Incorporate your opinions with your summary.

4 In small groups, take it in turns to present your summary and compare your opinions.

Language focus

Features of formal writing (Unit 1)

1 Rewrite these sentences so that they are expressed in a more cautious way.

1 Labelling is a reason people commit crime.
   Labelling is thought by some to be a possible reason people commit crime.

2 Culture is defined as the learned behaviour particular to one country or group of people.

3 The most effective leaders are those who take a strong, authoritative approach to management.

4 Motivation is the most important factor that impacts on language learning.

2 Rewrite these active sentences in the passive.

1 People who represent the forces of law and order create labels for others.
   Labels are created for people by the forces of law and order.

2 Good language learners show a natural aptitude for language learning.

3 Biology determines criminal behaviour.

4 The Western world causes most of the planet's pollution.

The Academic Word List (Unit 2)

3 Match each of the verbs (1–5) with its more formal equivalent (a–e).

1 get	**a** establish
2 use	**b** obtain
3 start	**c** ensure
4 need	**d** require
5 make certain	**e** consume

See pages 111–122 for further AWL practice

Word formation: suffixes (Unit 3)

4 Put the formal verbs from Exercise 3 (a–e) into this table and complete any gaps.

verb	noun	adjective
a establish	establishment	established
b		
c		
d		
e		

5 Complete these sentences using words from Exercise 4 in the correct form.

1 _____ of petrol and other fuels dramatically rose in the 20th century.

2 The company was _____ in America over 40 years ago and has been a major global company for more than a decade now.

3 Government policies reflect the importance many people now place on _____ fluency in a second language.

4 In many companies, it is a _____ for people to speak another language.

5 The financial results _____ that everyone's job was safe.

6 Complete each of the sentences below using the word in brackets and one of the prefixes from the box.

> mis–   mono–   re–   un–

1 After a difficult economic period, the company _____ (*established*) itself as a market leader.

2 The cultural _____ (*management*) of a situation could lead to the failure of a firm in a particular market.

3 It is not surprising that many people in the UK remain _____ (*lingual*), as little importance is placed on foreign-language learning.

4 Testing is seen as _____ (*important*) at a young age within some cultures.

7 Complete these sentences using the words in the boxes.

> whereas   furthermore

1 Motivation is considered to be an important factor affecting language learning, _____ it is not clear whether age impacts on success in language learning.

2 Motivation is considered to be an important factor affecting language learning. _____ intrinsic motivation can be especially important.

> additionally   however

3 Workers in Great Britain expect to have a certain amount of equality with their boss. _____ , they do not necessarily expect clear rules to follow.

4 Countries such as China and Japan place great importance on the present and the past; _____ in Great Britain, the emphasis is placed on the future.

Unit extension

1 **Look back through the book and make a note of new techniques you have learned. Add them to this table.**

I am confident I can use this technique.	I need further practice in this technique

2 **The Delta website (www.deltapublishing.co.uk) provides additional practice in all these skills. If you have not already used the files available, take a look and do some further practice.**

7 Culture

Aims

- Identifying text organization
- Identifying connected ideas
- Identifying bias, expertise and neutrality in a text
- Integrating sources and own ideas
- Identifying synonyms and pronoun referents

Topic focus

1 **Decide whether these statements are true (T) or false (F), then compare your answers with a partner.**

 1 Writing styles are the same all around the world.

 2 Academic writing is the same in all countries.

 3 Writing in an English-speaking university will be the same as in my country.

 4 Argumentation is common in all countries' academic writing.

 5 The type of source considered good to use is the same in all countries.

 6 Essay structure is the same in all countries.

2 **Have you noticed any differences between what would be considered good writing in your language and what is expected in English?**

3 a **Which of these points do you think are more important in forming an argument?**

 - the status and reputation of the author

 - appealing to the reader's values/emotions

 - logic and reason

 b **Which of these points do you think are more important in using external sources to use?**

 - historically important

 - acknowledging the source

 - using proverbs

 - recent studies

 c **Compare and discuss your responses with a partner.**

Understanding the text: text organization

 Understanding patterns or organization in a text helps to make the meaning clearer to the reader. It can help you identify main, supporting and contrasting ideas.

1 **Discuss these questions with a partner.**

　1　How can understanding the organization of the text help you understand the ideas in it?

　2　How many different methods of organization in a text can you think of?
　　　Example: time sequence

　3　Make a list of the different methods of organization that have been used in the texts in this book so far.
　　　Example

Text title	Structure(s) used
'Roles and purpose of assessment' (Unit 1)	Related ideas and examples

2 **Look at the texts in this book and complete this table with words that indicate each type of text organization.**

related ideas and examples	sequence	comparison/contrast
first, in addition	first, before	although, likewise
cause/effect	**problem/solution**	
leads to, is due to	problem, issue	

3 **Read the text on the next page, then answer these questions.**

Comprehension

　1　How does the author define coherence?

　2　How are ideas related in parallel progression?

　3　How are ideas related in sequential progression?

　4　How are ideas related in extended parallel progression?

　5　Does the author think one method is better than the others?

　6　When do problems occur?

Structure analysis

　7　What pattern of organization is used in this text?

　8　Underline language that helps you to identify this.

　9　What is the information related to the signal language you identified in question 8?
　　　Example: similar – compares the writing style with the running of a relay race (paragraph 2, line 1)

　10　Which method of text organization is common in your country?

Writing between cultures

Making sure that every piece of writing fits together is called *coherence*. Although there are different types of coherence, it is generally defined as the degree to which a document makes sense to the reader. Determining the effectiveness of coherence is a complex task because individual interpretation can vary. Author credibility, appeal to the reader's emotions and logic all inform the success of global coherence. Although global coherence is a difficult topic to examine, some of its mystery can be removed by analyzing three distinct versions – parallel progression, sequential progression and extended parallel progression.

Parallel progression is when the topic of successive sentences is the same. This is similar to a relay race, in which a runner passes a baton to the next runner. Like the transfer of a baton, parallel progression passes the topic of a sentence onto the next sentence. The result is a seamless exchange from beginning to end. This strategy demands less of the reader because the topic is always clear as it progresses within a paragraph. English-language writers follow parallel progression. The other two types of global coherence differ from parallel progression by their lack of connection between sentences.

Sequential progression appears more complex because topic transfer is not direct or obvious. Instead of handing a baton off to the next runner, the exchange is interrupted. The race continues, but it seems a little less direct. In actuality, writers from cultures using sequential progression see this type of writing as effective because it incorporates crucial details. From a sequential perspective, writers from cultures emphasizing parallel progression appear simple and obvious, whereas parallel-progression writers view sequential-progression documents as delayed and unfocused. While parallel progression and sequential progression are grounds for an endless source of confusion, there is also a third coherence strategy that combines both elements.

Extended parallel progression is when a document's introduction and conclusion are consistent, but are separated by a non-sequential body. In this respect, extended parallel progression combines elements of both parallel progression and sequential progression. The effect is one in which a claim is stated, shifts suddenly to a related but peripheral point, and then returns to the original claim. Russian, French and Spanish writers follow extended parallel progression.

All three types of global coherence begin and end with an implicit or explicit claim. But their paths are different. One strategy gives a sense that the argument proceeds directly from beginning to end. Another jumps from one sentence to the next, leaping from comment to topic. And a third strategy ties both ends of the text together with loose filler. The essential point behind these different writing strategies is that they are all examples of good writing. The problem comes when reading a document with different cultural assumptions.

Language focus 1: connected ideas

1 **Ideas in a text are often linked in three main ways. Discuss with a partner what you understand by each of these terms.**

   1 pronoun referents   2 synonyms   3 linking words

2 a **Look again at the text on page 61 and underline examples of pronoun referents. In each case, what does the pronoun referent refer to?**

   Example:
   pronoun referent: this (paragraph 2, sentence 2)
   referring to: parallel progression (paragraph 2, sentence 1)

   b **Circle examples of synonyms. In each case, what does the synonym refer to?**

   Example:
   synonym: this strategy
   referring to: passes the topic of a sentence onto the next sentence

   c **Draw a box around examples of linking words. In each case, what does the linking expression refer to?**

   Example:
   linking word: similar
   referring to: parallel progression and a relay race

3 **The language is very repetitive in this text. Working with a partner, use synonyms or pronoun referents to make it more varied.**

> The idea of plagiarism is common to all cultures; however, what exactly is or is not plagiarism varies from culture to culture. Buying an essay is likely to be seen as plagiarism in all cultures; however, not including an in-text reference may not be seen as plagiarism in all cultures. Not referencing a famous text may be seen as plagiarism in some cultures; however, in other cultures this would not be considered plagiarism and would be acceptable practice.

4 **In each of these sentences, there is a mistake with the linking word used. Work with a partner to correct the mistakes.**

   1 A clear main line of argument is important in some cultures; furthermore, it is not important in other cultures.

   2 Interactive seminars are not common in all cultures. In addition, they play a key role in many education systems.

   3 English is considered a global language; however, it has had a major impact on changing many cultures in the world.

   4 Culture impacts on writing styles, although it impacts on speaking styles.

For further work on pronoun referents, see Language focus 2 on page 67.

Critical thinking: bias, expertise and neutrality

 All claims or arguments need to be assessed, and one area they need to be assessed in is neutrality or bias. Is the author completely neutral, or do they have other reasons for making their claim, such as business or political motives?

Bias and neutrality 1 **Read this text and answer the questions below.**

> One report suggested that UK residents eating local lamb generated four times as many greenhouse gases as they would have, had they imported New Zealand lamb. But the study, whose funding by the New Zealand Lamb Export Association went unnoticed, only compared energy-intensive, industrial-agriculture methods in the two countries, and it never examined the greenhouse-gas impacts of local production.

1 Why is the author is concerned about the study related to New Zealand lamb?

2 Identify the section of the text where the author shows concern about the scope of the research.

3 Identify the section of the text where the author shows concern about neutrality or bias.

2 **Read this text and identify the possible bias in the claims.**

> In January 2007, Dannon introduced DanActive, described as a 'cultured probiotic dairy drink that has been clinically proven to help naturally strengthen the body's defense when consumed daily'. The company says in a statement that 'the scientifically substantiated benefits of Dannon's products are confirmed not only by the scientific journals that have reviewed and published the findings – which are made available on the company's websites for any and all to read – but also by the millions of highly satisfied consumers who enjoy Dannon's products'.

3 **Read this text and answer the questions below.**

> ● Blueberries, salmon, spinach and soy have all been hailed as 'superfoods' – foods rich in nutrients. Almost 100 products have been described as superfoods, and sales of products like blueberries and spinach have soared.

1 Who might make the above claims?

2 Who would you trust to make these claims?

4 **Work with a partner. Write a list of questions you could ask yourself to assess the neutrality or bias of a text.**

Examples: what is the background of the author?
who sponsored the study?

Expertise **5 Discuss these questions with a partner.**

1 How do you define the word *expert*?

2 How do you evaluate or decide whether somebody is considered an expert in their field?

3 Do you think old or modern sources are more important?

4 Can an expert ever be biased?

6 Read this text and answer the questions below.

Sources in different cultures

Finding and using references seems like the most basic of tasks associated with writing. Despite the universal need to support an argument with those who spoke before us, culture affects how authors credit their work. Some writers look for evidence and wisdom in old books, as passed down through literature over long periods of time. Yet other writers rely on different kind of support, one that is current and quantifiable. In China, for instance, writers are expected to use sources full of historical meaning. Confucius is as likely to appear in a paper on ethics as in a paper on business or medicine. Relying on ancient wisdom also indicates that the author is knowledgeable and educated. The problem occurs when a reader brings different assumptions about references, which may include a desire to minimize the use of historical texts in favour of more recent works. This is especially true of technical and scientific writing in Western cultures, two areas normally based on current and future innovations.

1 What does the text tell you about expertise in different cultures?

2 Can you always use old historic sources?

3 When are modern sources particularly useful?

> The Internet provides a wide range of sources, some of which are excellent for academic study. However, whilst not everyone can publish a book, anyone can write on the Internet. Therefore it is important to assess the author's expertise in an area before using a website in a piece of academic work.

7 a With a partner, write a list of criteria to evaluate expertise and reliability in these media.

- website
- newspaper
- book

Examples: Is the author an expert in their field?
How well researched is the writing?

b Share your ideas with another pair.

c How does selecting an expert text enhance your own writing?

Using the text: integrating ideas

1 **Two of the sections of each unit in this book are *Using the text* and *Critical thinking*. Discuss these questions with a partner.**

  1 What have been the main topics of *Using the text* so far?

  2 What have been the main topics of *Critical thinking* so far?

  3 How do you think *Using the text* and *Critical thinking* are connected?

2 **Work with a partner.**

  Student A: Look back at the texts in Units 1–3 and answer the questions below.

  Student B: Look back at the texts in Units 4–6 and answer the questions below.

  1 Underline the words that appear *before* each reference in the text. What is the function of these words?

  2 Circle the words that appear *after* each reference in the text. What is the function of each of these sentences?

3 **There are a number of phrases used to introduce a reference (e.g. *according to ...*). Work with a partner to make a list of phrases that are used to introduce references. Refer back to the texts in this book if necessary.**

  Phrases to introduce a reference

  according to

4 **Look at these two examples. Which one introduces the reference with caution?**

  a Welikala and Watkins (2008) claim that certain cultures encourage competition between learners and that therefore learners are less likely to positively respond to group work.

  b Welikala and Watkins (2008) state that certain cultures encourage competition between learners and that therefore learners are less likely to positively respond to group work.

5 a **Which of these phrases would you expect to argue for, which to argue against and which to be neutral? Write the phrases in italic in the correct column of the table below.**

  a Welikala and Watkins (2008) *claim* that the act of learning is not the same across all cultures.

  b Welikala and Watkins (2008) *point out* that the act of learning is not the same across all cultures.

  c Welikala and Watkins (2008) *argue* that the act of learning is not the same across all cultures.

argue for	argue against	neutral

Study tip
Different verbs indicate the line of argument; however, for some words such as *argue*, the line of argument may not be clear until the author comments on the quote afterwards.

  b **Add these words to the table above.**

  acknowledges   asserts   cautions   contends   defines
  describes   disputes   maintains   states

6 Read these three examples of references followed by comments. In which text does the author:

1 use another reference to criticize the first reference?

2 agree with the reference and become more specific?

3 add a further concern?

a

> Leask (2004) likens students' arrival at university to learning how to play a new game, where success depends on figuring out the new rules, applying them and 'winning' rewards such as good grades, positive feedback and a sense of confidence and competence as a learner. All students find learning the new university 'game' challenging, but international students may be doing so in English as a second, third or fourth language.

b

> Jin and Cortazzi (1999) observe that for Chinese students, few questions are spontaneous; students do not want to waste lecturers' time, and therefore questions are carefully considered before being articulated. In addition, for many students, their level of language development means that they will be translating from English to their first language and then back again.

c

> Oberg (1960) defines four clear stages an individual goes through before they can be considered fully adjusted to another culture. However, according to Bochner and Furnham (1982), these stages are not necessarily followed in a clear line, with people moving backwards and forwards between stages depending on the impact of events on the person's well-being.

7 Look at the quotes below related to this essay question. Develop each quote so that it is introduced and commented on.

> Writing styles are the same across all cultures. Discuss.

1 McCool (2009): Cultures do not write using the same assumptions, strategies and goals. These basic characteristics are of the utmost importance for someone writing in or for another culture.

2 McCool (2009): Writer responsibility is when the burden of communication is on the writer. Writer-responsible cultures emphasize clarity and concision, actions over nouns, practicality instead of theory, and a deductive chain of reasoning.

3 McCool (2009): Reader responsibility is when the burden of communication is on the reader. Reader-responsible cultures emphasize flowery and ornate prose, subjects over actions, theory instead of practice, and an inductive line of reasoning.

4 McCool (2009): Reader-responsible cultures interpret writer responsibility as obvious and simplistic, practical and narrow. Writer-responsible cultures interpret reader responsibility as poetic, excessively detailed, dismissive of practical implications, and broad and unfocused.

Language focus 2: pronoun referents

1 **In each of these sentences, what does the pronoun referent in italic refer to?**

  1 Learning is essentially cultural and social, as well as personal. *It* is informed by what acceptable knowledge is and how knowledge is communicated.

  2 In certain cultures, one of the main responsibilities of the teacher is to know the right answers and deliver *them* to the students.

  3 The role of a text varies between cultures. *It* can be seen solely as a source of knowledge or something to be questioned and challenged.

2 **Look at this passage. Make a list of each pronoun referent and the topic it refers to.**

> Because direct criticism is embarrassingly impolite or even politically dangerous in many cultures, expecting all students to feel at home critiquing authors they read is somewhat unrealistic. This problem is often more evident at graduate level than it is for undergraduates; first-year students from any culture often feel, quite rightly, that they don't have enough experience or information to evaluate critically what authorities in the field have to say. However, as they progress through the years, we expect that they do know enough – at least enough to venture an analysis of how carefully a study was constructed, how significant are the results of an experiment, how logical a theory is or how applicable in practice. But in cultures that are based on a stricter hierarchy, students feel – and are – subordinate longer; until they have credentials and status, their role is to accumulate information, not critique it.

Unit extension

Do an Internet search on the topic of 'adapting to different cultures'. Choose two sites and answer these questions.

1 Could you consider this source to be neutral, or is there an issue of bias?

2 Would you consider this an academic expert source? Why? / Why not?

3 How is the text organized? Is it sequential, comparing/contrasting, cause and effect, situation/problem?

4 Has the author incorporated quotes and/or references? How have they introduced these? How have they commented on these?

5 How are ideas connected? Look at linking expressions, synonyms and pronoun referents.

For further practice of the skills covered in this unit, go to www.deltapublishing.co.uk/resources.

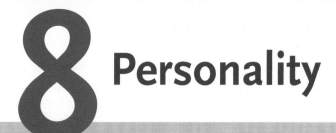

8 Personality

Aims

- Balancing speed and accuracy
- Noun collocations
- Identifying the significance of ideas
- Directly quoting in essays
- Analyzing noun phrases

Topic focus

1 **Work in pairs to match these adjectives to the jobs in the photos. You can match each adjective to more than one photo.**

athletic   careful   caring   creative   determined   hard-working
innovative   knowledgeable   patient   reliable   responsible   sociable
strict   ruthless   well-organized

2 **Answer these questions.**

1 Choose at least five adjectives to describe your own personality.

2 Look at your partner's personality description. Do you think the characteristics they have chosen would make them suitable for one particular job?

3 Would you say the adjectives you have chosen are how other people would describe you?

4 If you know your partner well enough, is this how you would describe them?

> ℹ️ In this unit, you are going to read a text on working in a team.
> Teamwork is important in both work and study, as it can impact on
> both your success and others.

3 **What do you think are the advantages and disadvantages of teamwork? Brainstorm your ideas with a partner.**

Understanding the text: speed vs. accuracy

> *i* It is important to balance speed and comprehension when reading. You need to choose a reading strategy that matches your reason for reading. For example, when deciding if a text is useful or not, a number of speed-reading techniques can be used; however, these techniques should not be used when detailed understanding is needed.

1 Work with a partner to answer these questions.

1 How many words do you think you can read in English in one minute?

2 What do you think is the average reading speed of a native speaker?

3 How can you improve your reading speed?

4 How can you best balance comprehension and speed?

2 a Look at these skills. In which unit did you practise each skill?

1 Identifying specific pieces of information

2 Thinking about who a book is written for

3 Ignoring unknown words

4 Using titles, chapter headings and subheadings

5 Identifying global meaning

6 Predicting content

b How often do you practise each of the above skills? Rate yourself on a scale of 1 to 5.

Never use this skill				Always use this skill
1	2	3	4	5

c Now rate your ability to use each skill.

Excellent				Poor
1	2	3	4	5

d Which of the skills aim to improve comprehension, and which focus on speed?

3 Look at the text on page 70. Try to read it as quickly as possible. Time yourself as you read. Calculate your words-per-minute reading speed.

Total words: 421

Time: _____

Words per minute: _____

4 Choose the correct answer for each of these questions without looking again at the text on page 70. Then check your answers with the text.

1 A good team is made up of _____ .
   a clever people   b similar personalities   c a variety of roles

2 There are _____ roles.
   a eight   b nine   c ten

3 Creative teams require _____ .
   a all roles from Belbin's list
   b a balance of roles from Belbin's list
   c a person with a sense of humour

4 People often have _____
   a a fixed team role   b nine team roles   c two team roles

One of the most popular and widely used analyses of individual roles within a work group or team is that developed by Meredith Belbin. Following years of research and empirical study, Belbin concludes that groups composed entirely of clever people or people with similar personalities display a number of negative results and lack creativity. The most consistently successful groups comprise a range of roles undertaken by various members. The constitution of the group itself is an important variable in its success. Initially, Belbin defined eight useful types of contribution – or team roles. A team role is described as a pattern of behaviour, characteristic of the way in which one team member interacts with another whose performance serves to facilitate the progress of the team as a whole. In a follow-up publication, Belbin discusses the continual evolution of team roles, which differ in a few respects from those originally identified, and adds a ninth role. Strength of contribution in any one role is commonly associated with particular weaknesses. These are called 'allowable weaknesses'. Members are seldom strong in all nine team roles. The nine roles are:

- Plant
- Resource investigator
- Co-ordinator
- Shaper
- Monitor–Evaluator
- Team worker
- Implementer
- Completer
- Specialist

The types of people identified are useful team members and form a comprehensive list. These are the key team roles and the primary characters for successful teams. Creative teams require a balance of all these roles and comprise members who have characteristics complementary to one another. 'No one's perfect, but a team can be.' Belbin claims that good examples of each type would prove adequate for any challenge, although not all types are necessarily needed. Other members may be welcome for their personal qualities, for example a sense of humour, but experience suggests there is no other team role that it would be useful to add.

The most consistently successful teams were mixed, with a balance of team roles. The role that a person undertakes in a group is not fixed and may change according to circumstances. Individuals may have a 'back-up team role' with which they have some affinity other than their primary team role. If certain roles were missing, members would call upon their back-up roles. Team roles differ from what Belbin calls 'function roles'. These are roles that members of a team perform in terms of the specifically technical demands placed upon them. Team members are typically chosen for functional roles on the basis of experience and not personal characteristics or aptitudes.

5 Write a list of criteria for you to improve your reading speed.

Example: ignore unknown words

> If you answered all the questions in Exercise 4 correctly, you can probably try to increase your reading speed. If you answered none of them correctly, you may need to slow down. It's important to balance speed and comprehension. Practise speed-reading regularly and you can quickly increase your speed.

Language focus 1: noun collocations

1 **Work with a partner to answer these questions.**

  1 What do you understand by the term *collocation*?

  2 Can you think of some common noun forms?
    Examples: *–ence, –ion*

2 **Look at the text on page 70 and underline anything you think is a noun or noun phrase. What words come before and after these nouns?**

3 **Match the nouns and noun phrases you underlined in Exercise 2 with the common collocation patterns shown in this table.**

structure	example
adjective + noun	*negative results, clever people*
noun + noun	*work group, team roles*
noun + preposition	*analyses of (individual roles), range of (roles)*
noun + relative clause	*team roles, which differ in a few respects from those originally identified*

4 **Answer these questions.**

  1 Which pattern from the table in Exercise 3 is used in each of these examples?
    a negative results
    b results which are negative
    c work group
    d a group which works together

  2 Which one(s) do you think are more likely in academic writing?

> Nouns and noun phrases are more common in academic writing than verbs and verb phrases. This is because more information can be packed into a shorter noun phrase.

> **Study tip**
> In academic writing, 'adjective + noun' or 'noun + noun' is more common than 'noun + relative clause'.

5 **a** **Look at these 'noun + relative clause' structures and find other noun phrases from the text on page 70 that mean the same.**

    1 a variable which was important   *an important variable*
    2 a role which is within a team
    3 a team which is creative
    4 a role which is used in back-up
    5 a demand which is technical

  b **Write three sentences using some of the noun phrases that you found.**

Critical thinking: interpreting the criticisms of others

1 Look back at the text on page 70 and discuss these questions with a partner.

> **Study tip**
> Many criticisms will already have been written about the theories and ideas of other people. Use these to inform and formulate your own criticisms.

1 What is your opinion of Belbin's work?

2 Can Belbin's claims simply be accepted or rejected?

3 What questions would you need to ask to accept or reject his claims, and why?
 Example: *What tests have been done to prove the theory? (without proof it is just an idea.)*

4 What opinions do you think people may have on Belbin's work?

2 Read this text which comments on the 'value' of Belbin's team-role inventory and underline the opinion of Furnham, Steel and Pendleton.

A study undertaken by Furnham, Steel and Pendleton had the aim of examining the psychometric properties of the Belbin Team Role Self-Perception Inventory. They believe (admittedly from very small samples) that there is little psychometric support for the structure of the inventories, which do not give confidence in the predictive or construct validity. In a response, Belbin argues that the inventory was a quick and useful way of intimating to readers what their own team roles might be; and Furnham, Steel and Pendleton acknowledge that Belbin's contribution is substantial and his measure imaginative.

Despite possible doubts about the value of Belbin's Self-Perception Inventory, it remains a popular means of examining and comparing team roles. For example, in order to explore whether local-government managers were distinctively different from the model of private-sector management, Arroba and Wedgwood-Oppenheim compared samples of the two groups of managers and Belbin's key team roles. There were noticeable similarities between the two groups, with the marked difference between private-sector managers and local-government officers in the score for team workers and the team roles they preferred to adopt. The individual characteristics of managers in the two sectors differed. The data implied that local-government officers were committed to organizational objectives and dedicated to task achievement, but the low score for team workers suggested the high commitment to organizational tasks was not supplemented by a concern for interpersonal processes. In local government, the drive and enthusiasm and emphasis on task completion were exaggerated, while attention to idea generation and productive interpersonal relationships was less marked.

Referring to the research of Belbin, White refers to a team in the proper sense of the word as something about the way they work as a group that adds up to a sum greater than the individual parts – a collective spirit, that makes them such a force. If businesspeople are happy to accept that group effort is always better than individuals working in isolation, the research of Belbin may help in constructing the perfect team. White suggests that, in the end, it is all about trust. The chances are that the dream team is out there, sitting opposite you or just round the corner. All you have to do is to fit them into Belbin's nine defined roles.

Using Belbin's model, Fisher et al. undertook a study of the distribution of team roles among managers. Over the past 15 years, many layers of management have been removed and the gap in people to lead and motivate has increasingly been filled by the creation of numerous teams. The participants of the study were 1,441 male and 355 female managers, all with some management experience. All had completed a personality questionnaire and were candidates short-listed for a range of management positions in both the private and public sectors. The study analyzed data supplied by ASE/NFER Publishing company, and results were compared with the Belbin model. The data broadly agreed with the Belbin model. The authors conclude that as much is still unknown about teams, it is reassuring that further support has been found for the popular Belbin team-role model. There are several unresolved problems with teamworking, but these might lie more with practices in staff recruitment than in team theory.

Identifying and understanding criticisms

3 a These phrases are key to understanding Furnham, Steel and Pendleton's opinion. Underline the part of each one that shows it is a criticism.

… there is little psychometric support …

… do not give confidence in the predictive or construct validity.

b Use your knowledge of word forms to work out the meaning of the rest of the two phrases above. Check your understanding with a dictionary.

c Underline the phrase in the text where Belbin defends his theory.

d Furnham, Steel and Pendleton reply that Belbin's contribution is *substantial and his measure imaginative*. How would you describe Furnham, Steel and Pendleton's opinion of Belbin's idea in your own words?

e What is the criticism that the author of the text makes of Furnham, Steel and Pendleton's work?

f What does this sentence from the text tell us about the significance of Belbin's idea?

Despite possible doubts about the value of Belbin's Self-Perception Inventory, it remains a popular means of examining and comparing team roles.

g Underline the two criticisms that White makes of Belbin's idea in the text.

h What is Fisher et al.'s position on Belbin? Underline the parts of the text that lead you to this conclusion.

> **ⓘ** Reading and interpreting criticisms of other people's work will help you to understand weaknesses in a theory. It will also help you to develop as a critical thinker and writer.

Study tip
The text in this section summarizes a number of questions or criticisms others have had of an individual's work. When reading a theory or idea, it is important that you engage in questioning the value or significance of claims made.

4 How would you summarize the significance of Belbin's idea? Think about these questions.

1 What criticisms of his idea are there?

2 How significant are these criticisms?

3 What support is there for Belbin's idea?

5 Write a brief summary that states the overall opinion of the importance of Belbin's work.

'They can't work as a team.'

Using the text: direct quotes

1 Discuss these questions with a partner.

1 What is the difference between an indirect quote and a direct quote?

2 When should you directly quote?

3 Which do you think is more common in an academic text, direct or indirect quotes? Look back at the texts in this unit. Which method is used more often?

2 Complete the definition of direct and indirect quotes below using the words and phrases in the box.

exact words   year and author surname   ideas   flexibility
the year, author surname and page   indirect quotes

An indirect quote uses the **1** _____ of another person but written with your own words. A direct quote uses the **2** _____ and ideas of the original author. An indirect quote includes the **3** _____ . A direct quote includes **4** _____ ; it also includes quotation marks. We directly quote an author when an idea is expressed so originally or is so well known that it is important to keep the wording. In general, **5** _____ are used more commonly because they give more **6** _____ in including the quote naturally within the text using the author's style of writing rather than the source's style of writing.

3 Look at this bibliography entry. What information would you need to include within the essay for an indirect quote?

Boddy, D. (2008) *Management: An introduction.* 4th ed. Harlow: Prentice Hall

4 Look at this extract from the essay in Unit 1 and answer the questions below.

One such form of this change is the use of peer and self-assessment. Self-assessment can be defined as 'the ability to critically assess one's own work' (Brew, 1999:160) and peer assessment as 'making judgments about, or commenting upon, each other's work' (Brew, 1999:160).

1 Why do you think the author has chosen to use a quote and not a paraphrase?

2 Which words come directly from Brew? How do you know this?

3 What does *1999* refer to?

4 What does *160* refer to?

5 Discuss these questions with a partner.

1 What do you think *et al.* means in the text on page 72?

2 Website authors are not always known. What should you write in this case?

3 Website years are also often unknown. What would you write in this situation?

4 Is there a difference in the following references?
   a According to Boddy (2008:10), '…'
   b In a recent study, Boddy (2008:10) found that …
   c '…' (Boddy, 2008:10)

Language focus 2: noun phrases

 In academic writing, it can be common for a noun to be influenced by a number of words that come before it.

1 **Look at these common language patterns. Can you find further examples of each pattern in the texts in this unit?**

adverb + adjective + noun	*very small samples*
adjective + noun + noun	*local-government managers*
adjective + adjective + noun	*productive interpersonal relationships*

 Many general English courses are based on 'grammar syllabuses'. In other words, they focus on teaching a variety of grammatical forms and structures. For example, at lower levels, you may learn present simple and continuous; at higher levels, past perfect simple and future continuous. As you have seen from this book, in academic writing, using a wide range of tenses is not common.

2 **Discuss these questions with a partner.**

1 Have you studied a grammar-based course before?

2 How might studying fewer tenses affect your learning and studying methods?

3 Do you think it is difficult to learn the same subject (e.g. English), perhaps after many years of study, with new aims and objectives?

Unit extension

Psychometric **was a term mentioned in one of this unit's texts. A psychometric test is a common method used to recruit somebody. It assesses their abilities and personality characteristics. Carry out the following research on psychometric testing.**

1 Find a definition of psychometric testing.

2 Assess the significance of psychometric testing as a recruitment method.

3 Find criticisms of psychometric testing as a recruitment tool.

4 Summarize the general view on psychometric testing in the literature you find. Think about these questions:

● Is it a key tool?

● What weaknesses does the technique have?

● Are some of the criticisms perhaps weak or unfair?

● Of all methods of recruitment – e.g. interviews, CV, assessment centre – how important or useful is psychometric testing considered to be?

For further practice of the skills covered in this unit, go to www.deltapublishing.co.uk/resources.

9 Ethics

Aims

- Identifying main ideas and supporting evidence
- Choosing between active and passive
- Using language to persuade
- Quoting indirectly and referencing in essays
- Verb collocation

Topic focus

1 **Look at the activities in the box and discuss the questions below with partner.**

> • copying a DVD   • downloading music without paying   • stealing a car
> • copying your friend's essay   • stealing fruit from an orchard

    1 Are all these activities acceptable behaviour?

    2 Which one is the most acceptable, and why?

    3 Which one is the least acceptable, and why?

2 **Read these situations and discuss the questions in Exercise 1 for them with your partner.**

    1 A company offers money privately to an individual to help get a contract for business.

    2 A company sponsors a political party's election campaign.

    3 Someone gives a job to their brother, even though other people were better qualified.

    4 Someone copies work from a friend and hands it in as their own work.

    5 Someone discovers a copy of the exam paper they will sit next week and takes it home.

    6 A company advertises an unhealthy food product to young people.

3 **Which of these factors influenced your opinion about the situations in Exercises 1 and 2?**

    ● parents   ● law   ● culture   ● age   ● gender   ● other

4 **Look at this essay question. How does it relate to the ideas you discussed in Exercises 1–3?**

> There are no common factors that make one group of people more or less likely to be unethical. Discuss.

Understanding the text:
main ideas and supporting evidence

1 **Discuss these questions with a partner.**

1 Are there factors that make one person more likely to be unethical, for example, nationality?

2 Who do you think is more likely to be unethical, a man or woman?

3 Do you think old or young people are more likely to be unethical?

4 Do you feel in control of your own destiny? Do you think this has an impact on your ethical behaviour?

2 **Read the text below and on page 78 to check your answers to Exercise 1.**

Individual influences on ethical decision-making

1 When people need to resolve ethical issues in their daily lives, they often base their decisions on their own values and principles of right or wrong. They generally learn these values and principles through their socialization process with family members, social groups and religion and in their formal education. The actions of specific individuals in scandal-plagued companies such as Enron, Worldcom, Halliburton, Qwest, Arthur Andersen and Aldelphia often raise questions about those individuals' personal character or integrity. They appear to operate in their own self-interest or in total disregard of the law and interests of society.

2 In the workplace, personal ethical issues typically involve honesty, conflicts of interest, discrimination, nepotism and theft of organizational resources. For example, many individuals make personal phone calls on company time. Most employees limit personal calls to a few minutes, and most companies probably overlook these as reasonable. Some employees, however, make personal calls in excess of 30 minutes, which companies are likely to view as excessive use of company time for personal reasons. The decision to use company time to make a personal phone call is an example of a personal ethical decision. It illustrates the fine line between what may be acceptable or unacceptable in a business environment. It also reflects how well an

3 individual will assume responsibilities in the work environment. Often this decision will depend on company policy and the corporate environment.

The way the public perceives individual ethics generally varies according to the profession in question. Telemarketers, car salespersons, advertising practitioners, stockbrokers and real-estate brokers are often perceived as having the lowest ethics. Research regarding individual factors that affect ethical awareness, judgement, intent and behaviour include gender, education, work experience, nationality, age and locus of control.

4 Extensive research has been done regarding the link between gender and ethical decision-making. The research shows that, in many aspects, there are no differences between men and women, but when differences are found, women are generally more ethical than men. By 'more ethical', we mean that women seem to be more sensitive to ethical scenarios and less tolerant of unethical actions. As more and more women work in managerial positions, these findings become increasingly significant.

5 Education, the number of years spent in pursuit of academic knowledge, is also a significant factor in the ethical decision-making process. The important thing to remember about education is that it does not reflect experience. Work is defined as the

number of years within a specific job, occupation and/or industry. Generally, the more education or work experience that one has, the better he or she is at ethical decision-making. The type of education has little or no effect on ethics. For example, it does not matter if you are a business student or a liberal arts student – you are pretty much the same in terms of ethical decision-making. Current research, however, does show that students are less ethical than businesspeople, which is likely to be because businesspeople have been exposed to more ethically challenging situations than students.

6   Nationality is the legal relationship between a person and the country in which he or she is born. Within the 21st century, nationality is being redefined by such things as the European Union (EU). When European students were asked their nationality, they are less likely to state where they were born than where they currently live. The same thing is happening in the United States, as someone born in Florida who lives in New York might consider him- or herself to be a New Yorker. Research about nationality and ethics appears to be significant in that it affects ethical decision-making; however, the true effect is somewhat hard to interpret. Because of cultural differences , it is impossible to state, for example, whether Belgians are more ethical than Nigerians. The fact is that the concept of nationality is in flux. The reality of today is that multinational companies look for businesspeople who can make decisions regardless of nationality. Perhaps in 20 years, nationality will no longer be an issue, in that the multinational's culture will replace the national status, a fact that can be seen in the number of young people in the European Union who are less likely to align themselves with a country and more open to the multinational EU concept.

7   Age is another individual factor that has been researched within business ethics. Several decades ago, we believed that age was positively correlated with ethical decision-making. In other words, the older you are, the more ethical you are. However, recent research suggests that there is probably a more complex relationship between ethics and age. As a result, we can no longer say 'the older, the wiser.'

8   Locus of control relates to individual differences in relation to a generalized belief about how one is affected by internal versus external events or reinforcements. In other words, the concept relates to where people view themselves in relation to power. Those who believe in external control (that is, externals) see themselves as going with the flow because that is all they can do. They believe that events in their lives are due to uncontrollable forces. They consider what they want to achieve depends on luck, chance and powerful people in their company. In addition, they believe that the probability of being able to control their lives by their own actions and efforts is low. Conversely, those who believe in internal control (that is, internals) believe that they control the events in their lives by their own effort and skill, viewing themselves as masters of their destinies and trusting in their capacity to influence their environment.

9   Current research suggests that we still cannot be sure how significant locus of control is in terms of ethical decision-making. One study found that a relationship between locus of control and ethical decision-making concluded that internals were positively related, whereas externals were negative. In other words, those who believe that their fate is in the hands of others were more ethical than those who believed that they formed their own destiny.

adapted from *Business ethics: Ethical decision-making and cases* by O.C. Ferrell, J. Fraedrich and L. Ferrell, 7th edition, South Western, 2009

3 a Read paragraphs 5–8 again and underline the main idea in each one.

b Underline the supporting details.

c Decide in each case if the support is further details, an explanation or an example.

4 Discuss with a partner how this text relates to the essay question on page 76.

5 Complete this table to show which ideas could be used in favour of, and which against, the statement in the essay question.

in favour of	against
Few studies show that there is a difference between men and women.	

6 a What other information would you need to be able to answer the essay question? Work with a partner to write three more research questions.

Example: Are the differences just between individuals?

b Compare your research questions with another pair.

Language focus 1: active vs. passive

1 Identify the subject, the verb and the object in these sentences.

  1 Employees bring certain traits and characteristics with them.

  2 Such factors were seized on in the aftermath of the corporate scandals of the early 2000s.

2 Work with a partner to answer these questions.

  1 Which sentence in Exercise 1 is passive, and which is active? Why?

  2 The passive is formed by the correct form of the verb *to be* and the past participle. Highlight the verb *to be* and the past participle in the passive sentence in Exercise 1.

3 Complete this table with the different forms of *to be* for the passive.

	verb *to be*	+ past participle
present	am/are/is	
present perfect		
past simple		
past perfect		
present continuous		broken
past continuous		
past perfect continuous		
infinitive		

4 Complete these rules with *what* and *who*.

  ● The passive is used when **1** _____ and not **2** _____ is more important.
  ● The active is used when **3** _____ and not **4** _____ is more important.

5 Complete these sentences with the correct form of *to be* and the past participle of the verb in brackets.

  1 Gender _____ the individual influence on ethical decision-making in business most often _____ (*subject*) to investigation.

  2 Students studying business subjects _____ (*find*) to be more unethical.

  3 Professional training and experience might also _____ (*consider*) to be important individual influences on ethical decision-making.

  4 The company's selection of employees _____ (*prove*) to be unethical.

6 Rewrite these sentences in the passive.

  1 Many people believe age is a factor in unethical behaviour.

  2 Many people regard nationality as a key influence on unethical behaviour.

  3 We interviewed ten people.

  4 Fifty people answered the questionnaire.

Study tip
The passive is commonly used in academic writing because the focus is on the idea more than the person who has the idea. It is also commonly used because it acknowledges that rarely is someone the first person to mention or discuss an idea. Finally, it can appear to be a less subjective form of writing.

Critical thinking: persuasive language

 Language can be used to persuade or lead the reader in the direction the writer wishes. It can be used to make the reader feel that there is no need to question an argument or that they are not normal for agreeing with the argument. It can also be used to influence people's emotions in response to an argument.

1 Match the different strategies used to persuade the reader (1–5) to the examples of these strategies (a–e).

1 emotive language

2 common belief

3 suggesting an idea is no longer relevant

4 suggesting an idea is beyond question

5 appeals to the group

a *obviously; of course; without doubt*

b *It is no longer the 19th century; times have moved on.*

c *It is commonly known that; It is widely accepted that; As we all know*

d *As educated citizens, it is normal to expect; No true American citizen would accept*

e *suffering; horrendous; harsh; inhumane*

2 Which argument strategy from Exercise 1 is being used in each of these extracts?

1 As everyone knows, gender influences many aspects of social behaviour, and ethical decision-making is no exception.

2 No right-minded British person would consider the government reforms to the welfare system to be ethical. It is part of the British system that all people are entitled to benefits and support if their financial situation requires it.

3 The conditions in which many old people are forced to live in Britain would not be considered acceptable in the Third World.

3 a Complete these sentences using phrases from Exercise 1. More than one answer is possible.

1 _____ any motivated person can learn a language well.

2 _____ we no longer work in such a hierarchical way.

3 _____ businesspeople are less ethical.

4 _____ we should be able to understand such arguments.

b If you use a different phrase, how does that change the meaning?

4 a Work with a partner. For each of these topics, choose a different style of persuasion and write a short text about the topic using that style.

- education
- leadership
- language learning
- sustainability
- crime

b Show your texts to another pair. Can you identify the style of persuasion being used in each?

1 **In this book so far, you have covered a number of topics that will help you to reference in an essay. Look back at previous units and list topics that may help, and how they could help.**

Example:

Method	How it can help
Summary writing	Allows a large amount of information to be shortened and included in a text

2 **What information from a source do you need to include with a direct/indirect quote?**

3 a **Underline the author and year in this extract.**

> Rarely are the differences found in the ethical decision-making of men and women (Ferrell, Fraedrich and Ferrell, 2009).

b **The page number is not included in the above extract. When should the page number be included?**

4 **Correct the mistakes the author has made in these quotes.**

1 Smith argues that governments are actually the most unethical organizations within most countries.

2 Johnson (1999) states that 'ethics can be defined as a fundamental belief that influences people's attitudes and behaviour'.

3 According to Zhang (2007:99), countries and companies, with a strict hierarchy, have their ethical behaviour determined by the head of the organization.

5 **Look at this reference. How is a quote from within another source recorded differently than one directly from the main source?**

According to McCabe (2007, cited in Smith, 2010), the group or organization has little influence on ethics in countries such as the UK and the USA.

6 **Find information in the text on pages 77–78 to support these ideas. Paraphrase or summarize the section you use and include an in-text reference.**

1 Age is not a clear indication of likely unethical behaviour.

2 Beliefs are less influenced by where we come from in today's global world.

7 The essay below was written in response to this question. Read it and answer the questions that follow.

> There are no common factors that make one group of people more or less likely to be unethical. Discuss.

1 What are the main arguments of the author?

2 Are these strong arguments?

3 How could they be improved?

Ethics as a field of study has a long history, with origins in the philosophies of Aristotle and Socrates. At a very basic level, ethics deals with good and evil, right and wrong, vice and virtue, and justice. Research has tried to identify what exactly makes one person more or less likely to behave unethically than another. This essay will argue that there are individual factors that make people more or less likely to behave in an unethical way and that these stem mainly from cultural backgrounds and not from more commonly researched backgrounds such as gender.

It is often stated that gender has a significant impact on the ethical decisions made by individuals; that, dependent solely on gender, decisions are likely to be more or less ethical, with the commonly held view that men are more likely to make unethical decisions. However, this is quite a simplistic view, as it does not take into consideration the wide and varied roles men and women can play in different cultures and contexts. Perhaps the more convincing argument is to look at it from the environment, specifically the culture, in which an individual grows up.

Each individual is heavily influenced by the cultural values of the country or society in which they grow up. Values and beliefs are formed by the society around us and can therefore be considered culturally rooted. As such, a person will decide if an act is right or wrong largely based upon the beliefs of that culture. For example, bribery is thought to be more or less acceptable, dependent on the country in which the act is committed.

In conclusion, factors such as age play a minor role in influencing how ethical decisions are made. However, culture creates the values and beliefs that form the window in which people view the world. As a result, culture can be said to greatly influence the ethical decision-making process.

8 Use the text on pages 77–78 to complete these tasks.

1 Find support for the main arguments in the essay above.

2 Decide if you will paraphrase or summarize the first idea you have selected.

3 Choose a phrase to introduce the reference.

4 Comment on the significance of the quote, e.g. What does it show? Why have you included it?

5 Choose another idea that you selected in task 1 and repeat tasks 2–4 for it.

6 Select where in the essay you would insert these references.

9 Discuss these questions with a partner.

1 What do you understand by *plagiarism*?

2 Think of at least four ways in which a student may plagiarize.

3 Plagiarism may not always be intentional. How might this happen?

Study tip
Applying these techniques will help you to achieve a number of key aspects of academic writing. In particular, to avoid plagiarism, to support your ideas and to critically comment on your quote.

Language focus 2: verb collocations

 Verbs collocating with prepositions are commonly used in passive structures in academic writing.

1 Complete the sentences below using the verb phrases from the box in the correct form.

associate with	focus on	influence by
investigate in	react to	refer to

1 A company's public image is .... its ethical behaviour.
2 Individual factors are .... much of the literature on ethics.
3 Although the influences of gender on ethical behaviour are often .... , there is actually little clear connection.
4 Orders of managers are .... differently, depending on the culture a person comes from.
5 Different nationalities are .... more strongly .... unethical behaviour.
6 Companies, governments and individuals are all .... in studies of ethical behaviour.

2 What preposition(s) do each of these verbs commonly collocate with?

1 benefit   2 write   3 provide   4 expose   5 respond   6 divide

3 Write a sentence using each of the collocations from Exercise 2.

Unit extension

1 Work on your own or with a partner to do these tasks.

1 Search for the word *ethics* in a variety of different sources such as academic books, journals, newspaper websites and organizations protecting people's rights.
2 Underline language you think is trying to influence the reader's opinion.
3 Is this language more common in one type of source? If so, what does this tell you about using this type of source?

2 Look at the same sources you used in Exercise 1 and do these tasks.

1 Underline the main idea in each paragraph.
2 Circle the supporting evidence.
3 Are main ideas supported in a similar way in the different texts?
4 Is the support interpreted in a similar way?

3 What can the type of language and support used tell you about the suitability of a text for use in academic writing?

For further practice of the skills covered in this unit, go to www.deltapublishing.co.uk/ resources.

10 Consumer behaviour

Aims

- Making claims and assumptions
- Language of comparison and contrast
- Summarizing agreements, definitions and propositions from multiple sources
- Evaluating evidence and argument
- Reporting

Topic focus

1 **Look at the photos on the left and discuss these questions with a partner.**

   1 What do you think is the main difference between each person?

   2 Which person is closest to you in age?

   3 Do you think there might be any similarities between you just because you are the same age?

2 **Work in small groups. Think about your generation, your parents' generation and your grandparents' generation. Think of words or phrases to describe their beliefs, behaviour and attitude, and use them to complete this diagram.**

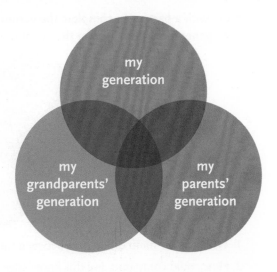

> ℹ Companies often group people together into consumer groups in order to target a larger group with their marketing. This is done because it is assumed that people of a similar group will behave in a similar way when making purchases. One way to group people is by generation.

3 **What do you think are differences in the shopping behaviour of the three groups in Exercise 2?**

   Examples: Typical products purchased, method of shopping, money available to spend

Understanding the text: claims and assumptions

 A *claim* can be seen as the main argument in a text. An *assumption* is an unspoken claim. It is something that the writer is assuming the reader will accept without evidence and is the link between the reason and conclusion. As you read a text, identifying underlying assumptions can help you to understand the writer's main argument.

1 a **Read this example and the possible underlying assumption below.**

Extract from a text on marketing: *The over-50s in the UK hold 80% of the country's wealth and 40% of spending power. It is not only the only segment that is growing, but also the one that has more disposable income than all the others combined (Cummins, 1994; Bond, 1997).*

Possible underlying assumption:
- That the over-50s segment is an important market. It has a lot of money and could be very profitable for a company; also, they would spend money rather than save it.

b **What possible assumptions could be made about this situation?**

The over-50s enjoyed cheap house prices in comparison to today. Therefore many people bought a house.

2 **The text on pages 87–88 describes three different generations. Does the text include any topics from your discussion on page 85?**

3 **Look at the footnotes in paragraph 2. Then read paragraph 3 and identify a) any claims made; and b) any underlying assumptions.**

4 **Work with a partner to complete the various segments of this diagram summarizing each generation, then answer the questions below.**

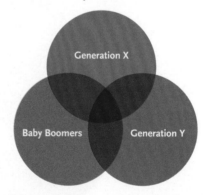

1 What are the main differences between the generations?

2 How could companies use this knowledge?

5 **Answer these questions.**

1 How many different types of age are defined in the text?

2 Why does the author believe it is important to understand the different generations?

3 Which was the first generational cohort to be recognized?

4 What two things have particularly influenced Generation Y?

5 Why is Generation X a difficult group for marketers?

6 Why are the Baby Boomers more attractive than previous generations?

7 What makes the over-50s such a popular market today?

8 Is the chronological or cognitive age lower in the Baby Boomers?

Consumer behaviour: Generations

1 Rather than looking at the issue of age from only a chronological perspective, we can combine chronological age with other age perceptions (e.g. biological age, social age, cognitive age, subjective age, personal age). This means biologically we have a physical age; psychologically we grow, learn and mature through what we learn and our experiences, and socially we develop as a result of our interaction with others, from family to peer and reference group (Treguer, 2002).

2 The approach, then, is to consider how those from specific 'generations' behave as consumers. Each cohort will have gone through the same era and will have had similar experiences during their formative years as adults.[1] A major implication of the generational cohort approach is that marketers are given clues as to what to say to each cohort segment, and how to say it, on the basis of the formative events experienced within each cohort.[2] Indeed, Belk (1988) has asserted that 'possessions are a convenient means of storing the memories and feelings that attach our sense of past', and in this way the consumption patterns of generational cohorts can be predicated on important symbolism.[3]

3 A major generational cohort, and in some sense the first to be recognized as such, was the generation born in the years following the Second World War; that is, between 1945 and 1965. This explains the subsequent divisions of generations based on a 20-year generational span (i.e. allowing individual development to about age 20) and the mid-decade periods. However, we 'work backwards' here, from the most recent adult/young generation, those born between 1977 and 1994.

4 **Generation Y (or 'N').** Those born between 1977 and 1994 have been termed Generation Y or the Millennium Generation (Adam Smith Institute, 1998). Sometimes this cohort is labelled the 'N-Gen' after the Net and the information revolution which have had such a major impact on their development (Schewe and Meredith, 2004). Many in this category have been found to be materialistic, brand-orientated risk-takers who are keen on business, hedonism and illegal drugs. They have also been found to have a disrespect for politics. But they are not as cynical as their predecessors, Generation X. The Future Foundation (2000) extended this research and found Generation Y to be more accepting of multinationals and less interested in protesting. Further analysis of Generation Y has been conducted by Shepherdson (2000) and Gofton (2001). If this group were targeted by marketeers, this profile could provide useful clues as to the sort of message and media to use and reach them. Davidson (2003) describes them as being introspectively and self-expressively motivated:

'They are only interested in their personal lives, parties they go to, the clothes they wear … the absence of community … the cult of celebrity provides an exciting surrogate community … celebrity provides a real identity in a sea of mock individuality.'

5 **Generation X (or 'Baby Busters').** This group was born approximately between 1966 and 1976, and the name 'Generation X' was coined by Coupland (1991). Indeed, he probably started the sequence of 'alphabetical' generations, because Gen X was the first so-labelled back in the early 1990s. They have become important consumers – demanding their own products and searching for their own identity. A complicating factor is that this group has been found to be especially individualistic and sceptical of marketing activity. O'Donohoe and Tynan (1998), for example, found that young adults are indeed marketing literate. This doesn't make them difficult to reach, but it is proving harder to influence them. Coupland (1991), Bashford (2000) and Ritchie (1995) have analyzed their behaviour and attitudes. Ritchie, for example, declares that 'Xers' have known much more advertising all their lives, compared with older generations, but that they do not 'dislike advertising … they dislike hype … overstatement, self-importance, hypocrisy and the assumption that anyone would want to be disturbed at home by a salesman on the telephone'. Research International (1996) also found these young adults (by then in their 20s) to be dismissive of advertising that insults intelligence, knocks competitors or tries too hard to be 'hip'.

6 Xers might also be more interested in engaging with marketing rather than being passive receivers of it. If so, marketing can provide some of what Generation X might be looking for – that is, greater interactivity and participation in marketing communications. Indeed, in their interpretation of their research in 35 countries, Research International (1996) suggested that practical implications of the young adult perspective would lead to 'interactive, challenging relationships' between advertiser and consumer.

7 **Baby Boomers.** We turn now to consider the first of the generational cohorts identified as such, those born between 1945 and 1965. The Baby Boomers – those born in the years following the Second World War – have very distinctive attributes and have become a very important target for marketers. They were involved in a massive social revolution which changed music, fashions, political thought and social attitudes for ever (Fifield, 2002). They were the generation to grow up in the 1960s when the term 'teenager' hadn't previously been used. They were not 'small adults' who, in previous generations, had worn

---

1 There is the assumption that just because someone is born at the same time, they will have the same experiences.
2 There is the assumption that all people born in the same era can be persuaded in the same way.

3 There is the assumption that people a) buy particular products because of their age, and b) associate memories with products.

similar clothes to their parents. The new generation, however, wanted their own culture, their own fashions and music, and their own social attitudes, which ejected the values of their parents. In addition to these desires, the Baby-Boomer generation was also the most affluent of any 'youth market' until their era, so they were able to engage in the consumer market, and marketers responded with a fashion and music explosion which we had not previously experienced.

8 This cohort is now turning 50 and there are 20 million people aged over 50 in the UK, and this figure will approach 25 million by 2021 (Ahmad, 2002). Such a consumerism-literate market should be extremely attractive. Indeed, in the USA, a Baby Boomer turned 50 every 6.8 seconds in 2001. The large segment coupled with its purchasing power – it was the first to become empowered as consumers – means it is a favourite target for marketers.

9 Overall, they are relatively wealthy, in terms of inheritance from their parents. That previous generation was 'blessed' with low house prices when they bought and a lifestyle which was much less materialistic. As a result, their estates have often (but clearly not always) been cascading down to the new over-50s market. Many have a 'cognitive age' less than their 'chronological age' and therefore act much more youthfully than their age might suggest (Szmigin and Carrigan, 2000, 2001). In other words, they have a youthful self-concept.

Language focus 1: comparison and contrast

1 **Look back at the text above. How would you describe its structure? Does it evaluate, compare and contrast, follow time order, suggest solutions to a problem?**

2 **Which of these definitions corresponds to *evaluate*, and which to *compare/contrast*?**

   a to judge the importance, value, quality or significance of something

   b to look at similarities and/or differences between two or more things

3 **Circle the parts of the text that evaluate and underline those that compare.**

4 **Look at the parts you underlined in Exercise 3. What language is used to make the comparison or contrast? Make a list of words or phrases used to make comparisons and contrasts.**

   Examples: more, less

5 **Think of other phrases for comparison and add them to your list from Exercise 4. Are all the phrases formal?**

6 **Complete these sentences using comparative expressions. You can use the ideas from the text to help you.**

   1 Generation Y is _____ materialistic than the generations before it.

   2 Generation Y is _____ open to other cultures.

   3 The generation before the Baby Boomers were known as 'little adults', _____ the Baby Boomers were known as 'teenagers'.

   4 It is easy to reach Generation Xers with advertising; however, it is _____ difficult to influence them.

7 **Look at this essay question. Use the text from this unit to write down your initial ideas.**

> Describe the main differences between Generation Y, Generation X and the Baby Boomers.

Using the text: summarizing from multiple sources

1 **Read the text on pages 87–88 again. Which of the following best summarizes the author's main purpose?**

   a To describe the different generations

   b To show how generations influence consumer behaviour

   c To argue that age has little impact on consumer behaviour

2 **Read paragraph 4 again and answer these questions.**

   1 What is the author's main idea?

   2 How many of the sentences are referenced to another author?

   3 What is the relationship between the main idea and each reference?
      Example: Reference 1: giving a time period to the group

3 **Look at this reference and answer the questions below.**

   Baby Boomers have been described as mentally younger than their biological age (Szmigin and Carrigan, 2000, 2001; Preel, 2000; Treguer, 2002).

   1 Why do you think there are so many different names and years after the source?

   2 What do you think is the reason for including so many references?

   > *i* Whilst researching for an essay, you will often find opinions or evidence that oppose each other. You will often also find evidence and opinions that are similar to each other in a number of different sources. Combining these opinions can strengthen an argument, as it shows a number of studies or experts hold the same view.

4 **Which sentence in the Generation Y section is this quote most similar to? Does it add a similar point or contradict a point already made in the paragraph?**

   Generally described as optimistic, team-orientated, high-achieving rule-followers, the millennials have driven down suicide rates, violent crime and drug use. (Howe and Strauss, 2003).

5 a **Summarize and reference these two definitions of a Baby Boomer and their era in one short text.**

   Gibson (1993) has suggested that the Baby Boomers' adulthood has, uniquely, been characterized by dramatic social changes, including the women's movement, an increasingly technological and service-orientated workforce and the shift to a global economy.

   The Baby Boom generation blamed their parents for being too rigid and excessively strict in the parent–child relationship and complained of a lack of freedom in numerous areas of their daily life (Treguer, 2002).

   b **Compare your summary and reference with a partner.**

Critical thinking: evaluating evidence

1 a Give the main focus of each of the topics covered in critical thinking so far in this book.

topic	main focus
Identifying viewpoint	to find the main opinion of the author
Questions to help analyze texts	
Distinguishing fact from opinion	
Isolating reasons and conclusions	
Cause and connection	
Bias, expertise and neutrality	
Significance	
Persuasion through argument	

b Which ones mainly focus on weakness of argument?

2 Discuss these questions with a partner.

1 What type of evidence can be used to support an argument?
Examples: quotes, statistics ...

2 Other than the examples discussed in Exercise 1, how can evidence be weak?

3 A *sample* is a small section of the people a research project intends to investigate. Why do you think samples are used?

4 What needs to be considered when selecting a sample?

3 These are four additional areas you need to consider when evaluating evidence used to support a claim. Match each area (1–4) to its definition (a–d).

1 relevance   a The number of people that took part in the research

2 sample size   b If the sample used to reach a conclusion is too small

3 overgeneralization   c A group of people who characterize the entire population of the research project

4 representative samples   d Proof that is clearly related to the topic

4 Read this paragraph and answer the questions below.

Baby Boomers have the most money available to spend of any generation. According to Bond (1997), the over-50s in the UK hold 80% of the wealth and 40% of the spending power. Therefore, Baby Boomers are likely to spend large amounts of money on their children.

'Run! 73 million Baby Boomers are about to retire!'

1 Is the evidence relevant to the conclusion drawn?

2 Does it follow logically?

3 Are there any underlying assumptions?

4 Could a different conclusion be reached on the same evidence?

5 Read these five extracts. For each one, look at the evidence used to support its conclusions. Is the evidence strong, or, if there is a weakness, what type of weakness is it?

1

> The over-50s are an important market for the tourist industry. According to the Telegraph group (1999), people aged between 55 and 64 take more holidays than average, and more than half are planning two or more holidays in the next 12 months. Therefore, this could be a very profitable market to target.

Possible weaknesses: It might actually be those over 65 that take the most holidays and spend the most money; we don't know how many people were surveyed; we don't know other data such as social class which may have an influence.

2

> Research has shown that Generation Y is obsessed with celebrity culture. Smith (2009) interviewed 100 respondents, of which 85% agreed that they would like to become rich and famous. As a result, television programmes offering normal people the chance to become famous for singing are likely to continue to be popular.

3

> The need for autonomy and independence has been cited as one of the main causes of divorce in Generation X. A men's magazine questioned more than 50,000 readers, of which nearly 30% agreed that they wanted to leave their wife because they felt trapped and wanted independence.

4

> Credit cards are commonly used by the over-50s. In a survey of over-50s consumer spending, Cummins (1994) found that the largest group (21%) use credit cards to spend more than they can actually afford.

5

> Encouraging customers to remain loyal is key to the growth and development of any business. According to Cooper (2003), young customers tend to change their product loyalty very quickly, whereas mature consumers tend to be more loyal. Therefore, marketing campaigns should be targeted at the older generation rather than the younger one.

6 Which of these is the main weakness of the text on pages 87–88?

a relevance

b sample size

c overgeneralization

d representative samples

7 Write a checklist you could use in future to help you analyze the strength of argument presented in a source.

How many people were involved in the study?

Language focus 2: reporting

1 a **Look back at the text on pages 87–88 and find verbs that relate to the ideas of others.**

b **Use some of the verbs to complete these sentences.**

1 People born between 1945 and 1965 _____ the Baby Boomers.

2 Smith and Watson have _____ further, but have not found conclusive support.

3 The study _____ age is the most influential criteria for determining consumer behaviour.

2 **What is the corresponding noun for each of these reporting verbs?**

1 argue   2 describe   3 explain   4 imply   5 state

3 **Rewrite these sentences using the noun form of the words from Exercise 2. Start with the phrases given.**

1 Tindal argues that social class has a greater influence on consumer behaviour than age.
   Tindal puts forward the ...

2 Whilst Bell uses generation cohorts to explain much of a consumers' behaviour, this does not take into account a number of other factors.
   Bell's ...

3 Fisher describes consumer behaviour as the way consumers interact with the buying process.
   Fisher ...

4 **Create your own sentences using the two other verbs from Exercise 2 in their noun form.**

Unit extension

1 **Research the topic of consumer behaviour or another academic topic that interests you. Find a topic that has developed over time, but be quite specific (for example, *Gender influences on consumer behaviour*). As you read your sources, take notes and think about the following.**

- Which ideas build on previous ideas?
- Which ideas have looked at the same idea from a different perspective?
- Which ideas support each other?
- Which ideas counter each other?

2 **Write a paragraph showing how each of these ideas are interlinked.**

For further practice of the skills covered in this unit, go to www.deltapublishing.co.uk/ resources.

3 **Often textbooks will already provide a summary of a field that has been studied by many people. Find two or three such summaries on the same topic by different authors and compare how they summarize the topic.**

11 Nutrition

Aims

- Drawing conclusions
- Language of cause and effect
- Using bibliographies and references
- Statistics
- Language that describes graphs

Topic focus

80% of British men overweight by 2022

25% of all deaths in the US occur from heart attacks

1 Discuss these questions with a partner.

1 Who is the oldest person you know?

2 What do you think has helped them live to such an old age?

3 Some countries have a much higher life expectancy than others. Why do you think that is?

4 Look at the headlines above. Do you think the focus of these articles will be to persuade or inform?

5 Do you think statistics are used more commonly to inform or persuade?

2 Look at these headlines and discuss the questions below.

Chewing gum improves concentration and learning

Eating fruit and veg does not reduce the risk of cancer

Average life expectancy increases by 5 hours every day in the UK

Passive smoking kills 600,000 every year

Half-hour walk a day keeps you healthy and sane

1 Do you think these headlines are true?

2 In the UK, such headlines are quite common. How common are they in your country?

3 Why do you think such stories are so popular?

1 a Work with a partner to decide which of these are possible functions of a conclusion.

1 To make future predictions

2 To summarize the main idea

3 To include something new and different to the main body

4 To draw arguments together logically

5 To restate the main argument

6 To leave ideas open for the reader to interpret

7 To relate back to the essay question

8 To make conclusions about a wider area than the essay question

b Where would you expect to find conclusions?

Example: at the end of a chapter

> Unspoken conclusions are similar in some ways to assumptions. However, assumptions link the reason and conclusion; unspoken conclusions are made from a series of points that lead us to a conclusion. They can be more persuasive than a stated argument, as these are often analyzed in more detail because they are clearly stated.

2 Read the text on page 95 and answer these questions.

1 Does the author believe diets and lifestyles have changed?

2 What reasons does the author give for increases in obesity?

3 What environmental factors have had the biggest impact on obesity?

4 Does everybody agree that genetics play a role in obesity?

5 Does the author believe genetics play a role in obesity?

3 Match these conclusions to the appropriate paragraph.

1 Lifestyle definitely plays a role in obesity, and genetics might do. paragraph 1

2 Genes may play a role in obesity, but it is not clear how.

3 Eating too much and exercising too little is a basic factor in obesity, but not the sole reason.

4 The recent rapid increase in obesity around the world is due to the environment, but individual differences may be genetic.

5 The fact that people live in a similar environment but are of a different weight may be so because of genetics.

6 The constant, cheap supply of food is one main environmental cause.

4 a Read paragraph 4 carefully. Answer this question, then compare your answer with a partner.

What conclusions could be made on the basis of this paragraph?

b Does this paragraph mainly help to draw conclusions about the environment or genetics?

5 Read paragraph 5 carefully and answer these questions.

1 Why has the author used a twin study rather than studies of a family?

2 Do all twins grow up in the same environment?

Obesity – environmental or genetic?

1 Few would deny that obesity is one of the major health problems facing the world today (Maziak et al., 2007). However, what the main causes of obesity are and how the situation can best be managed are issues that cause much discussion. Whilst at a basic level it is clear that there is an imbalance in energy consumption and expenditure, it is not clear to what extent genetics and the environment play a role in rising levels of obesity (Prentice and Jebb, 2005). It is also unclear why this imbalance has increased at the speed and extent that it has (Friedman and Schwartz, 2008).

2 The basic energy-balance equation comes from the relationship between energy in and energy out. The number of calories each food provides will depend on the food type; for example, a gram of protein or carbohydrate contributes four calories to our energy in, whilst a gram of fat equates to nine calories. In terms of energy expenditure, three factors need to be considered: the basal metabolic rate (BMR), the energy used for physical activity, and the thermic effect of food. The BMR is the amount of energy the body needs to perform basic functions such as beating the heart and regulating body temperature. The thermic effect of food is the energy needed to digest the food we consume. A simple and apparently obvious link to the cause of obesity is an imbalance between the amount of energy consumed and the amount expended. However, this is a common misconception, as the relationship is more complex than this, and genetic and environmental factors also need to be considered.

3 According to O'Rahilly and Farooqi (2006), when we consider the causes of lifestyle-related obesity, we need to break it down into two common factors. First of all, there is the mass global expansion of obesity in recent years, with numbers more than doubling since 1980 (WHO, 2011). Such a rapid change over a short period of time suggests that environmental rather than genetic factors have contributed, as genetic change happens much more slowly. The second factor to consider is individual differences within a subpopulation. Largely speaking, these individuals will be exposed to similar environmental factors, but there will be a range of individuals from slim to obese. In a similar environment, differences are more likely to be explained by genetic differences.

4 From an environmental perspective, the most significant changes in the last century have been shown to be in the supply, consumption and choice of food. Tillotson (2003) argues that there have been two factors that have contributed to major changes in food supply in the last century. Firstly, that industrialization increased the range of food available; and secondly, that knowledge of nutrition rapidly increased. In addition to these changes, which were often supported by economic or political policies (Hoek and McClean, 2010), there have been significant changes in the retail sector. In many developed countries, the retailing of food products is dominated by a small number of companies. This has changed both the range of products accessible and the amount of food available throughout the year. It has also given significant power to companies to influence consumer choice through marketing and pricing strategies. Drewnowski and Darmon (2005) found that healthier food products such as lean meats and fish were more expensive than energy-dense foods such as fats and sugars. Therefore, these environmental changes, along with a more sedentary lifestyle, could explain the general mass worldwide increase in obesity levels.

5 Many individuals claim to have a genetic disposition to obesity. However, unlike environmental issues, this is a more widely contested area. According to Yang et al. (2007), a review of the literature into the area of genetics and obesity shows that although several genes may predispose individuals to weight gain, their impact is limited. However, in studies of identical and non-identical twins, Maes et al. (1997) found that the genetic contribution to individual weight differences was higher in identical twins, possibly resulting in 50–90% of the total. This connection decreases with age, as environmental factors start to play a more significant role (Hewitt, 1997). Whilst studies appear to indicate some connection, what is not known at this stage is which genes are having an impact and the extent of each gene's influence.

6 It is clear that there is no one cause of obesity and that many factors have led to the situation the world faces today. The genetic and environment debate is likely to continue until we fully understand the role of individual genes and their connection to obesity. However, it can be concluded that the worldwide increase, in such a short period of time, is largely due to environmental changes, as the genetic make-up of humans cannot have significantly changed in such a time frame. However, when considering differences within individuals in a particular population, the reasons could be genetic.

Language focus 1: cause and effect

1 a **Find these expressions in the text on page 95. What ideas do they connect?**

   1 link to   **2** shown to   **3** contributed to

b **Complete this table with other expressions related to cause and effect.**

adverbs and conjunctions	verbs	nouns
therefore, because	shown to, link to, contribute to	effect of

c **Choose one word or phrase from each column and write a cause–effect sentence related to diet. Exchange your sentences with a partner. Do you think your partner has used the expressions correctly?**

2 **Complete the verb phrases below using the prepositions in the box. Use the definitions in brackets to help you.**

by   for   of   of   to   to   to   to

   1 account _____ (to explain the cause or reason for something)
   2 attribute _____ (to say that something or someone is the reason for something)
   3 because _____ (as a result of something)
   4 cause _____ (the reason why something has happened)
   5 caused _____ (the thing or person responsible for the result)
   6 contribute _____ (to help to cause an event or situation, not always the main reason)
   7 lead _____ (can result in something)
   8 owing _____ (a reason for something)

3 **Complete these sentences using phrases from Exercise 2. You may need to change the grammatical form.**

   1 The increased inactivity of people in the Western world in part _____ the increasing levels of obesity.
   2 The influence of a Western diet on much of the world is often claimed to be the _____ increasing weight issues in many countries.
   3 The predicted fall in life expectancy is _____ diet and weight.
   4 The risk of cancer can increase _____ an increased consumption of alcohol and cigarettes.
   5 The _____ an increased life expectancy are not fully clear.

Using the text: bibliographies and references

1 a **Mark the statement(s) that describe your approach to research.**

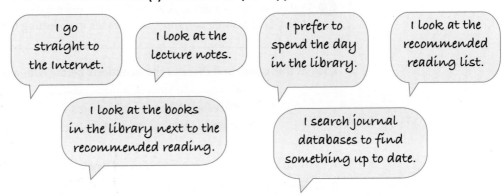

b **Once you have a source, how can you use this to lead you to other sources?**

2 **Look at passage below from a source text. Imagine you had to write this essay, and answer the questions that follow.**

> Evaluate the impact of a variety of factors on the increase of obesity in the UK.

1 Which other source might be the most useful to read?

2 What additional information would you need to locate this source? Where would you find this?

Obesity in the UK

The UK has seen a significant increase in the proportion of obese people, with approximately one in four people considered to be obese (Johnson, 2009). A number of individuals cite their genetics as the main contributory factor; however, there is little evidence to support this (Smith, 2008). There is an increasing body of research analyzing the root causes of obesity and the possible consequences to society. In terms of the causes, Pearson et al. (2010) found that one of the main contributory factors was likely to be the increased sedentary lifestyle that has become more prevalent in the last 20 years.

3 **Look at the bibliography below and answer these questions.**

1 Who wrote *Fat economics: Nutrition, health and economics*?

2 What is the title of the book by Webb?

3 Why are there two titles in the book published in 2010?

4 Who published *Nutrition: A health promotion approach*?

Dytham, C. (2003) *Choosing and using statistics: A biologist's guide*. 2nd ed. Oxford: Wiley-Blackwell
Friel, S. and Lichacz, L. (2010) *Explaining patterns of convenience food consumption*. In G. Lawrence, K. Lyons and T. Wallington *Food security, nutrition and sustainability*. London: Earthscan
Lim, M.Y. (2007) *Metabolism and nutrition*. 3rd ed. London: Mosby/Elsevier
Mazzocchi, M. (2009) *Fat economics: Nutrition, health and economics*. Oxford: Oxford University Press
Webb, G.P. (2008) *Nutrition: A health promotion approach*. 3rd ed. London: Hodder Arnold

4 a **Look at this essay question. Which of the books in Exercise 3 could be useful?**

> Discuss the wider impact of obesity on society. Which areas other than the health system is it impacting upon?

b **Compare your answer with a partner.**

Critical thinking: statistics

 In this section, we will look at some of the main difficulties of understanding statistics and some common weaknesses in collecting them.

1 Look at this quote and discuss the questions below with a partner.

> There are three kinds of lies:
> lies, damned lies, and statistics.

1 Why do you think this person believes lies and statistics are the same thing?
2 Do you agree with the quote?

2 Read the text below and answer these questions.

1 When did statistics start to become important?
2 Why did statistics become important?
3 What are the two purposes of statistics?
4 What do we need to question about statistics?

During the nineteenth century, statistics – numeric statements about social life – became an authoritative way to describe social problems. There was growing respect for science, and statistics offered a way to bring authority of science to debates about social policy. In fact, this had been the main goal of the first statisticians – they wanted to study society through counting and use the results to influence social policy. They succeeded; statistics gained widespread acceptance as the best way to measure social problems. But, beginning in the nineteenth century and continuing through today, social statistics have had two purposes: one public, the other often hidden. Their public purpose is to give an accurate, true description of society. But people also use statistics to support particular views abut social problems. Numbers are created and repeated because they supply ammunition for political struggles, and this political purpose is often hidden behind assertions that numbers, simply because they are numbers, must be correct. People use statistics to support particular points of view, and it's naïve simply to accept numbers as accurate, without examining who is using them, and why.

3 a Complete these definitions using the words and phrases in the box.

innumeracy	official statistics	social problems

1 Crime rates, unemployment rates, poverty rates are all _____ .
2 _____ is a label we give to a social condition, and it is that label that turns a condition into something we consider troubling.
3 _____ is a mathematical equivalent of illiteracy. Just as some people cannot read or read poorly, many people have trouble thinking clearly about numbers.

b Discuss with a partner what the weakness of each might be.

Example: Social problems can be 'created' by the government so that they can be seen to be actively solving the issue, or they could be 'created' by the media to sell newspapers.

4 Use the questions in the Study tip on page 98 to make criticisms of each of these paragraphs.

1 The Chief of Police today delivered the news that official statistics for crime are showing a decline in some key areas targeted by government policy. Recent crime statistics show that for the third consecutive year, since the election of the new government, overall levels of crime have fallen by 10%.

Who created this statistic?
The police and/or a government agency is most likely to have created this statistic.

Why was this statistic created?
This is an official statistic, so it might have been created to show that a government policy is working.

How was this statistic created?
This statistic shows the overall picture, but does not consider the type of crime. Some crimes may be up, perhaps even more serious crimes. Perhaps minor crimes have become so frequent that people do not report them. Therefore, this statistic was created to show an overall favourable picture and not necessarily the true and detailed picture.

2 Old people in the UK continue to be affected by the increasing prices for fuel, with some depressing and devastating results. Last year, 25,000 more people aged over 75 died in the UK over winter, compared to other periods of the year. Today, the government announced it will protect elderly people's financial benefits to help them pay for heating.

3 For the first time in centuries, life expectancy is actually falling rather than rising. This is the first generation that is expected to live a shorter life than their parents, and the root cause of this is the fact that 25% of the population are considered to be obese.

5 If you are cynical about something, you tend to not to believe it is true or that people are only interested in themselves. Discuss these questions with a partner.

1 In the UK, people are quite cynical of newspapers. Why do you think this is?

2 Are people in your country cynical of the press?

3 In the UK, people are also often cynical of politicians. Why might this be the case?

Language focus 2: describing graphs

1 **Work with a partner. Do a quick sketch of what you think each of these charts would look like.**

    1 bar chart   **2** pie chart   **3** flow chart   **4** table   **5** line graph

2 **Match each of these words which can be used to describe a graph (1–4) to its definition (a–d).**

    1 label   **a** describes what each part shows

    2 key   **b** the vertical and horizontal lines on the sides of a graph

    3 axes (sing. axis)   **c** describes what each axis shows

    4 bar   **d** a solid horizontal or vertical block used in a chart to show an amount

3 **Give the corresponding noun form for each of these verbs describing a movement or trend.**

    1 drop   **2** decline   **3** fall   **4** grow   **5** rise   **6** increase   **7** decrease

4 *In* **and** *of* **are the main prepositions that collocate with the nouns you found in Exercise 3. How are they used differently in these phrases with** *drop***? (Hint: What type of information follows each preposition?)**

    a a drop **of** 1% in the level of obesity in children

    b a drop **in** the level of obesity in children

5 **What words can you think of to describe the size or speed of movement?**

    Example: a sharp rise in sales
                     Sales fell dramatically.

6 **Find a graph showing changes in obesity levels either in your country or in the world. Use the words and phrases from this section to write a brief description of the graph.**

Unit extension

1 **Choose one of the topics covered in this book, such as Education, Sustainability or Crime, and do these tasks.**

    1 Find newspaper articles that present statistics related to your chosen topic.

    2 Analyze the statistics and decide how reliable you think they are.

    3 If the article you found mentions other sources, find them. Do these sources help to strengthen the original article? How?

    4 What conclusions could you make on the basis of your research?

2 **Do some research for this essay question.**

> Describe and exemplify situations where statistics can be considered reliable.

For further practice of the skills covered in this unit, go to www.deltapublishing.co.uk/resources.

12 Revision

Understanding the text

Speed vs. Accuracy (Unit 8)

1 List three strategies you could use to help you read the text on pages 102–103 quickly.

2 Read the text quickly, timing yourself. Note down your time and work out your reading speed in words per minute.

Text length:	668 words
Time:	....
Words per minute:	....

Study tip
You should ideally be aiming for 200 words per minute or more.

3 Without looking at the text, choose the correct answer to each of these questions.

1 How many classifications did the original model have?
   a six   **b** eight   **c** seven

2 Which of the following is not true?
   a The social-grade system is simple to research.
   b The social-grade system is often a good indicator of consumer behaviour.
   c The social-grade system is no longer used.

3 Which of the following was *not* a criticism of the research?
   a Lower social grades often earn more money than some higher social grades.
   b People make decisions on the basis of more than social grade.
   c Forty-one per cent of all respondents were given the wrong social class.

4 The new system studies …
   a individuals.   **b** families.   **c** over 75s.

Text organization (Unit 7)

4 How many main types of text organization are there?

Example: time sequence

5 a Look at the text on pages 102–103. What type of text organization is used here? Underline language that indicates this pattern.

b Compare your answers with a partner.

6 a Look at the text again and do these tasks.

  1 Underline the main idea in each paragraph.

  2 Circle the supporting details.

  3 In each case, decide if the support is further details, an explanation or an example.

b Compare your answers with a partner.

7 Match each of these terms (1–2) to its definition (a–b).

  1 a claim

  2 an assumption

  a something which the writer thinks the reader will accept without evidence and which is the link between the reason and conclusion

  b the main argument in a text

8 Why is it important to notice claims and assumptions in texts?

9 Underline the claim and circle the assumption in each of these two paragraphs.

  1 First, it is simple to research. All that is required is for data to be analyzed according to the occupation of the 'chief income earner in the household'.

  2 It has also been shown that of 400 respondents to earlier surveys who were re-interviewed to confirm their social grade, 41% had been allocated to the wrong group, and this is an indication of instability of the system.

10 The text below highlights some of the weaknesses in the assumptions underlying the social-grade system. What are they?

  Example: Everyone in the same grade will have a similar income.

11 a Many of the paragraphs in the text below leave a possible unspoken conclusion. What unspoken conclusion could you make for paragraphs 2–7?

  Example: Paragraph 2: Different purchasing patterns create opportunities for businesses to exploit.

b Compare your ideas with a partner.

Consumer behaviour: Social class

1 Especially in the past, marketers have acknowledged that there is a degree of social stratification, but they have long avoided researching possible segments on the basis of social class in any true sociological sense. This would involve rather complicated assessment of income, wealth, power and skill.

2 In the UK, instead of this, social grade is determined via the occupation of the 'chief income earner' in the household. A sixfold classification results: A, B, C1, C2, D, E. The main 'dividing line' is between C1 and C2, above which there are non-manual occupations and below which there are manual ones (Market Research Society, 2004). Many commercial market-research programmes have found significant differences in buying behaviour between respondents in the various social grades.

3 The traditional justification for the continued use of grade is basically twofold (Market Research Society, 1981). First, it is simple to research. All that is required is for data to be analyzed according to the occupation of the 'chief income earner in the household'. Second, social grade appears to have been a reasonably good discriminator of buying behaviour, as you will find in many (but not all) product-markets profiled in MINTEL-style reports. Social grade also reflects lifestyle patterns and is used widely by advertisers while profiling customers.

4 During the 1980s in particular, a number of significant criticisms of social grade were made. There are inevitable anomalies for its use. For example, significant proportions of those earning above the national average are C2DE, so the traditional strong correlations between social grade and income have been destroyed. Some in C2, such as highly skilled manual workers, will be earning more than middle managers in group B, and some full-time students in C1 will be earning less than some manual workers in D.

5 It has also been shown that of 400 respondents to earlier surveys who were re-interviewed to confirm their social grade, 41% had been allocated to the wrong group, and this is an indication of instability of the system (O'Brien and Ford, 1988).

6 Another problem concerning social grade is that although there might be some correlations between social grade and purchase, how can this be used? Certainly it is relevant for selecting appropriate advertising media based on the matching of segment social grade with the social-grade profiles for different media. But there could be dangers in inferring values and attitudes of those in each social grade in order to create marketing communications messages. These more affective dimensions might not be caused by occupation. Furthermore, in the context of the urban industrialized environments, where social networks can be complex and fluid in nature, it is often difficult to think of a group of consumers as a community of individuals who are bound together by a common social grade or social status (Henry, 2005).

7 Recent attempts to improve social classification do not bode well either. The census of 2001 has produced eight (rather than the previous six) categories, but excludes the over-75s (Zelin, 2003). Indeed, the new system has been found to be as good a discriminator of purchase activity as the 'ABC1' system, but Rose (1999) could not recommend it as a replacement for social grade. However, the previous system was based on households (occupation of chief income earner in the household), whereas the new system is at individual level, so the marketer might be tempted to at least experiment with this because of the stronger potential of data at individual level. However, in comparative research, the Market Research Society (2004) concluded that the old social-grade model was a better discriminator than the new socio-economic classification (SEC) and indeed the latter 'would have none of the advantages we would look for in a new system' (Market Research Society, 2004). It is, therefore, perhaps not surprising that the 2001 census output included both the new SEC and the standard (ABC1) social gradings (Market Research Society, 2004); but maybe it is surprising that it attracts such criticism in itself.

Critical thinking

Bias, expertise and neutrality (Unit 7)

1 List five ways in which research and claims can be biased, and give an example of each.

2 a Define *expert*. How are experts viewed in your country? Do you think they are viewed in the same way in other countries?

   b Compare your answers with a partner.

Significance (Unit 8)

3 a Look back at the text on pages 102–103 and underline the parts that highlight the significance of social grades.

   b Now identify the parts of the text that criticize the claimed significance.

4 a Look again at the text on generations in Unit 10 (pages 87–88) and compare the significance of generations and social grades as marketing tools.

   b Which do you think is more commonly used, and why?

   c Compare your answers with a partner.

Persuasion through language (Unit 9)

5 This table shows five forms of persuasion through language. Work with a partner to add more expressions to the table.

emotive language	suffering
common belief	obviously
suggesting an idea is no longer relevant	It is no longer the 19th century.
suggesting an idea is beyond question	It is commonly known that …
appeals to the group	As educated citizens, it is normal to expect …

Evaluating evidence (Unit 10)

6 a In the text on pages 102–103, which paragraph uses statistics to make a claim?

   b How is this used as evidence to make a claim?

   c What is the weakness in this evidence and its related claim?

7 a Look at paragraph 7 in the text on pages 102–103. The author criticizes other people's and organization's claims. Underline the claims and circle the criticism.

   b What language is used to counter the claims?

   Example: However, …

I think we'd both be happier if you worked somewhere else, Darren …

A great coach provides honest and constructive feedback, even when it's not what the other person wants to hear …

www.CartoonStock.com

Using the text

Integrating other's ideas with your own (Unit 7)

1 **Match each of the quotes below (1–3) to the correct description of the author's view of it (a–c).**

 a The author is neutral about the idea.

 b The author will argue against the idea.

 c The author will support the idea.

 1 Belbin (1993) defines nine distinct team roles.

 2 Belbin maintains that the inventory is a quick and useful way of intimating to readers what their own team roles might be.

 3 Furnham, Steel and Pendleton dispute the roles defined by Belbin and claim that there is little psychometric support for the structure of the inventories.

2 **Match each of the extracts below (1–3) to the correct description of it (a–c).**

 a It uses another reference to criticize the first reference.

 b It agrees with the reference and becomes more specific.

 c It adds a further concern.

1

> Furnham, Steel and Pendleton acknowledge that Belbin's contribution is substantial and his measure imaginative. Despite possible doubts about the value of Belbin's Self-Perception Inventory, it remains a popular means of examining and comparing team roles. For example, in order to explore whether local-government managers were distinctively different from the model of private-sector management, Arroba and Wedgwood-Oppenheim compared samples of the two groups of managers and Belbin's key team roles. The individual characteristics of managers in the two sectors differed. In local government, the drive and enthusiasm and emphasis on task completion were exaggerated, while attention to idea-generation and productive interpersonal relationships was less marked.

2

> A study undertaken by Furnham, Steel and Pendleton had the aim of examining the psychometric properties of the Belbin Team-Role Self-Perception Inventory. They believe (admittedly from very small samples) that there is little psychometric support for the structure of the inventories, which do not give confidence in the predictive or construct validity. In a response, Belbin argues that the inventory was a quick and useful way of intimating to readers what their own team roles might be

3

> The authors conclude that as much is still unknown about teams, it is reassuring that further support has been found for the popular Belbin team-role model. There are several unresolved problems with teamworking, but these might lie more with practices in staff recruitment than in team theory.

Direct quotations (Unit 8)   **3 a Which of these is an example of a direct quote?**

   a According to Jones (2008:54), 'Statistics that are largely social should always be approached with caution.'

   b According to Jones (2008), social statistics should be used cautiously.

b Do you think such a quote needs to be direct, or would it be suitable as an indirect quote? Why?

4 Select part of the text below to support this opinion with a direct quote.

Gender is not a key factor in ethical decision-making.

> A good place to start in examining the individual influences on ethical decision-making is to consider some basic demographic factors, such as age and gender. For example, one common question is whether men or women are more ethical. This is no doubt an interesting question, and according to O'Fallon and Butterfield (2005), gender has been the individual influence on ethical decision-making in business most often subjected to investigation. However, overall, the results have been less than conclusive, with different studies offering contradictory results, and often no differences found at all (Loe et al., 2000; O'Fallon and Butterfield, 2005). For example, half of the studies reported by Ford and Richardson (1994) conclude that women are more ethical than men, whilst half suggest no difference.
>
> (Crane, 2007:136)

Indirect quotations (Unit 9)   **5 What factors do you need to consider when indirectly quoting?**

Example: The quote is directly relevant to the opinion being expressed.

6 a Look at this opinion and do tasks 1–4 below.

Baby Boomers were the first generation to be defined as significantly different to the previous generation.

   1 Find support for the opinion above in the text below and on the next page.

   2 Decide if you will paraphrase or summarize the idea you have selected.

   3 Choose a phrase to introduce the reference and use this bibliographic information to show the source:
   Evans, M., Jamal, A. and Foxhall, G. (2006) *Consumer behaviour.* Chichester: Wiley and Sons Ltd

   4 Comment on the significance of the quote, e.g. What does it show? Why have you included it?

b Choose another reference from within the text on pages 87–88. Do tasks 1–4 above for it.

> **Baby Boomers.** The Baby Boomers – those born in the years following the Second World War – have very distinctive attributes and have become a very important target for marketers. They were involved in a massive social revolution which changed music, fashions, political thought and social attitudes for ever (Fifield, 2002). They were the generation to grow up in the 1960s when the term 'teenager' hadn't previously been used. They were not 'small adults' who, in previous generations, had worn similar clothes to

their parents. The new generation, however, wanted their own culture, their own fashions and music, and their own social attitudes. In addition to these desires, the Baby Boomer generation was also the most affluent of any 'youth market' until their era. Overall, they are relatively wealthy, in terms of inheritance from their parents. That previous generation was 'blessed' with low house prices when they bought and a lifestyle which was much less materialistic. Many have a 'cognitive age' less than their 'chronological age' and therefore act much more youthfully than their age might suggest.

Summarizing from multiple sources (Unit 10)

7 a Look at the paragraph below. Underline sentences that are original to the author and circle quotes used.

b What is the relationship between each quote?

Example: Quote 1 introduces the concept of gender and ethics

A good place to start in examining the individual influences on ethical decision-making is to consider some basic demographic factors, such as age and gender. For example, one common question is whether men or women are more ethical. This is no doubt an interesting question, and according to O'Fallon and Butterfield (2005), gender has been the individual influence on ethical decision-making in business most often subjected to investigation. However, overall the results have been less than conclusive, with different studies offering contradictory results, and often no differences found at all (Loe et al., 2000; O'Fallon and Butterfield, 2005). For example, half of the studies reported by Ford and Richardson (1994) conclude that women are more ethical than men, whilst half suggest no difference.

Language focus

Connected ideas (Unit 7) 1 a **Read the text below and find words to complete the left-hand column of the table.**

b **For each word you have written in the table, write the connected idea in the right-hand column.**

	connected idea
pronoun referents *us*	*you and me*
synonyms	
linking words	

What is it about you or me that makes us act in a particular way when confronted by an ethical problem? Clearly all employees bring certain traits and characteristics with them into an organization, and these are likely to influence the way in which the employee thinks and behaves in response to ethical dilemmas. Although this could be taken to suggest that some people are simply more ethical than others, this is rather too simplistic a view. Individual factors can also account for why some people are perhaps more swayed than others into unethical conduct because of the influence of their colleagues. Similarly, individual factors can explain why some people perceive particular actions to be unethical, whilst others do not. Over the years, researchers have identified a number of important individual influences and their likely influence on ethical decision-making.

Noun phrases (Unit 8) 2 **Identify noun collocation patterns in the text on pages 102–103 and complete this table.**

structure	example
adjective + noun	
noun + noun	
noun + preposition	
noun + relative clause	

3 **Choose one example of each structure in Exercise 2 and write an example sentence.**

Verb collocation (Unit 9) **4 Complete the sentences below with the 'verb + preposition' collocations from the box. The collocations all appear in the text on pages 102–103, so look back to check if you are not sure of the meaning.**

allocated to	appear to	based on	found in	profiled in

1 Social classifications are _____ the main income earner of the household.

2 Social classifications _____ be a good indicator of consumer behaviour.

3 One weakness of the system is that social grade is not always a good indicator of income. Higher income earners can be _____ lower social classes.

4 The typical consumer _____ the study showed that gender is an additional factor in consumer behaviour.

5 People are _____ a social class based on the main income of the household.

5 Find other 'verb + preposition' collocations in the other texts in this unit. Try to work out their meaning and create your own sentences with them.

Comparing and contrasting (Unit 10) **6 Divide the following into words/phrases for similarity and words/phrases for differences.**

In the same way   On the other hand   While   Similarly   Like   In contrast

Neither … nor   Both   Whereas   Whilst

7 Connect each of these pairs of sentences with a word or phrase from Exercise 6.

1 Baby Boomers were called 'teenagers'. Their parents at the same age were called 'small adults'.

2 Students are in social grade C1. Middle managers are in social grade B.

3 Someone from northern Europe and America might be more likely to reflect on ethical problems alone in order to make their own independent decisions. Someone from a culture such as Southern Europe and Latin America might be more likely to consult a wider group. A high power-distance culture like Japan or China might be less willing to question the orders given by their superiors, even if they felt they were being asked to do something unethical.

Cause and effect (Unit 11) **8 Complete the sentences below with the prepositions in the box.**

for	from	to	to	to

1 Understanding consumer behaviour is a reason _____ the development of social classifications.

2 Increased obesity has given rise _____ increased numbers of heart attacks.

3 Obesity can lead _____ higher levels of diabetes.

4 High life expectancy in Japan is often attributed _____ a healthy diet.

5 Problems with heath can often arise _____ dietary issues.

9 Think of three more cause-and-effect phrases and create your own sentences.

Unit extension

1 Look back through the book and identify five skills that you would like to practise more.

2 Find texts related to your current or future studies and use them to practise the five skills you identified in Exercise 1.

3 Bring your texts and practice exercises to the next class. Swap your work with a partner and evaluate the effectiveness with which your partner has completed the tasks they set themselves.

Academic Word List exercises

Unit 1

1 Match the words (1–10) to their definitions (a–j).

1 assess	a an opinion that unfairly supports a person or thing, often influenced by personal opinion
2 bias	
3 criteria	b to give a score or mark to work
4 grade	c to show or make known
5 indicate	d a series of steps or actions leading to a particular end
6 issue	
7 method	e to judge the value, importance or quality of something
8 process	
9 select	f to choose carefully, often a small number of things
10 structure	
	g the way in which something is organized
	h the standards used to judge something
	i a way of doing something
	j a problem or subject that causes discussion

2 Complete this table with the different forms of words from Exercise 1.

verb	noun	adjective	adverb
assess	1	assessable assessed	
	bias	2	
3	grade	gradable graded	
indicate	indication	4 .... indicated	indicatively
5	issue	issued	
methodize	method methodization	6 .... methodized	7 ....
process	process processability	8 .... processable	
select	9	selected selective selectable	selectively
10	structure	structured	

3 Complete each of these sentences with the word in brackets in the correct form.

1 The work was .... (*grade*) by the teacher.
2 The marks were not .... (*indicate*) of the student's ability.
3 The results were checked .... (*method*).
4 The university is very .... (*select*) about which students it will take.
5 The exam was .... (*structure*) to include short answers and essays.

4 Match each set of words (1–5) to the words (a–e) to form collocations.

1 impact / extent / effectiveness
2 towards / against / heavily
3 satisfy / fulfil / set of
4 raise / address / major
5 slow / methodical / mental

a process
b assess
c biased
d criteria
e issue

5 Complete each of these sentences with a collocation from Exercise 4.

1 How much of a problem will the scandal involving the minister cause? We need to assess the .... of the damage.
2 It is important when conducting scientific experiments to follow a .... process.
3 The newspaper is .... biased in favour of the leading political party.
4 Prior to starting an assessment, students are shown a .... criteria used to mark the assessment.
5 The essay received a low mark because it did not .... the issue of the question.

Unit 2

1 Match the words (1–10) to their definitions (a–j).

1	achieve	a	a group of people who work together to do something
2	corporation	b	a large company or group of companies
3	committed	c	aim; something you want to achieve the future
4	goal	d	can avoid harm from any danger or threat
5	involve	e	loyal and happy to give your energy and time to something you believe in
6	secure	f	out of 100, shown by the symbol %
7	per cent	g	position that someone/something has in relation to others
8	status	h	to include or employ somebody/something in an activity
9	style	i	to succeed in doing something through hard work
10	team	j	way of doing something

2 Complete this table with the different forms of words from Exercise 1.

verb	noun	adjective	adverb
achieve	1 _____	achievable achieved	
	corporation	2 _____	
commit	3 _____	committed	
involve	4 _____	involved 5 _____	
secure	security	secure secured	6 _____
	per cent percentage	7 _____	
8 _____	style	styled 9 _____ 10 _____	stylishly

3 Complete each of these sentences with the word in brackets in the correct form.

1 The scientists discovered a cure for one of the most common viruses in existence – it was an amazing _____ (achieve).

2 It has been suggested that achieving good reading skills in small children requires heavy _____ (involve) from the parents.

3 Employees are likely to feel demotivated if their jobs are not _____ (secure).

4 Creating a _____ (style) advert can help a brand of perfume to be successful.

5 It is well known that students need to show a certain level of _____ (commit) to their subject if they are to achieve good grades.

4 Match each set of words (1–5) to the words (a–e) to form collocations.

1 culture / identity / hospitality

2 long-term / short-term / ultimate

3 high / low / small

4 social / high / low

5 member / leader / effort

a percentage

b goal

c corporate

d status

e team

5 Complete each of these sentences with a collocation from Exercise 4.

1 Hotels and health spas make a lot of money as a result of corporate _____ .

2 Every _____ of the team is expected to actively participate in meetings and to respect the decisions made by management.

3 An extremely _____ percentage of British males are considered to be overweight, and this is one of the reasons that a large number of British men over 50 suffer from heart problems.

4 Many people purchase high-end products, such as sports cars, in order improve their _____ status amongst their friends and colleagues.

5 The manager was criticized for only thinking about _____ goals – he only cared about what the company would be doing next year and didn't think about the situation ten years from now.

Unit 3

1 Match the words (1–10) to their definitions (a–j).

1	conduct	**a**	facts, numbers or information
2	data	**b**	meaning 'no' or 'not positive'
3	evidence	**c**	to perform and organize an activity
4	negative	**d**	meaning 'yes' or 'not negative'
5	neutral	**e**	not supporting either side
6	period	**f**	detailed study of something
7	positive	**g**	a person who provides a response or reply
8	research	**h**	a general change or development in a situation or behaviour
9	respondent	**i**	a reason or reasons to believe something is or is not true
10	trend	**j**	a phase of time, often long

2 Complete this table with the different forms of words from Exercise 1.

verb	noun	adjective	adverb
conduct	1	conducting	
	evidence	2	evidently
negate	negation	negative	3 ....
4	neutralization	neutral	neutrally
	period	5	periodically
6	research		
7	respondent response	8	9 ....
	trend	10	

3 Complete each of these sentences with the word in brackets in the correct form.

1 It was .... (*evidence*) from the test results that the project was not a success.

2 It is unhelpful for team members to show a .... (*negate*) attitude whenever change is proposed.

3 Whenever conflict occurs between two team members, it is important that management stays .... (*neutral*) wherever possible.

4 The systems are updated .... (*period*).

5 We had an excellent .... (*respond*) to our survey.

4 Match each set of words (1–5) to the words (a–e) to form collocations.

1 recent / downward / economic

2 attitude / result / effect

3 experimental / historical / statistical

4 a survey / an experiment / an interview

5 conduct / do / undertake

a conduct

b data

c positive

d research

e trend

5 Complete each of these sentences with a collocation from Exercise 4.

1 Employers always look for people who have a positive .... towards their company's products.

2 The archaeologists were able to extract a large amount of .... data at the site of the old school.

3 Sales of hybrid cars have only increased in the last few years, so this is a relatively .... trend.

4 An .... was conducted, and the Oxford graduate was given the job.

6 Replace the words or phrases in italics with collocations from Exercise 4 in the correct form.

1 The *numbers continuing to fall* in car sales has shown no signs of stopping.

2 An increase in salary only has a *good impact* for a short period of time.

3 The *old figures* suggest that the winner in this region is likely to be the overall winner at the end.

4 *A test was done* to establish consumer attitudes towards the changes.

7 The collocations *conduct/do/undertake research* are all similar in meaning, but two are considered more formal. Which ones do you think they are?

8 Use words from the exercises on this page to create five sentences on the topic of this unit.

Unit 4

1 Match the words (1–10) to their definitions (a–j).

1 attitude
2 aware
3 benefit
4 consume
5 domestic
6 economy
7 energy
8 role
9 sustain
10 transform

a to know that something exists
b to use something such as fuel, energy or time, or to eat something
c power from sources such as oil and electricity
d to help someone or to be helped by something
e to continue for a period of time
f the trade and industry systems of a country
g to change significantly
h an opinion or belief about someone or something
i a function or purpose someone or something has, particularly in a company or organization
j relating to a person's country, house or home

2 Complete this table with the different forms of words from Exercise 1.

verb	noun	adjective	adverb
	1	aware	
benefit	benefit benefactor	2	beneficially
consume	consumption 3	consumed consumable	
domesticate	domesticity	domestic	4 ....
economize	economy	5 .... 6	economically
energize	energy	energetic	7 ....
sustain	sustainability	sustainable 8	sustainably
transform	transformation	transformable 9	

3 Complete each of these sentences with the word in brackets in the correct form.

1 It is not considered to be .... (*benefit*) for children to start school before the age of four.

2 The .... (*consume*) of energy worldwide has increased dramatically in recent years.

3 As more and more evidence points towards the inevitability of global warming, more and more companies have to consider the issue of .... (*sustain*).

4 The new management team needed to .... (*transform*) the image of the company in order for it to be successful again.

5 Following a war, a country's .... (*economic*) situation is usually fairly unfavourable.

4 Match each set of words (1–5) to the words (a–e) to form collocations.

1 nuclear / solar / renewable
2 active / important / dual
3 well / environmentally / politically
4 policy / market / affairs
5 positive / negative / towards

a attitude
b aware
c domestic
d energy
e role

5 Complete each of these sentences with a collocation from Exercise 4.

1 .... energy is not generally considered to be viable in cold countries.

2 The company was experiencing falling sales in overseas markets, but their domestic .... was still strong.

3 All British schoolchildren learn about climate change, so most of them are extremely .... aware.

4 He displayed an extremely .... attitude towards the new product during the meeting and, as a consequence, he was given a written warning by his manager.

5 Many European women now have a .... role, as both homemakers and career women.

Unit 5

1 Match the words (1–10) to their definitions (a–j).

1 conclude
2 define
3 environment
4 factor
5 identify
6 individual
7 interact
8 label
9 link
10 theory

a to explain the meaning or limits of something

b a situation that influences the result of something

c to communicate with or react to

d a connection

e the air, water and land that people, plants and animals live in

f ideas to explain a fact or event

g a word or a phrase to describe the characteristics of people, activities or things

h to recognize someone/something, a problem, a fact, etc.

i a single person or thing

j to end a piece of writing or a speech

2 Complete this table with the different forms of words from Exercise 1.

verb	noun	adjective	adverb
conclude	conclusion	1	conclusively
define	definition	2 .... defined	
	environment	environmental	3 ....
identify	4 .... 5	identifiable	identifiably
	individual individualism individuality individualist	6 .... individualistic	individually
interact	interaction	7	interactively
8	label	labelled	
9	link	linked	
10	theory	theoretical	theoretically

3 Complete each of these sentences with the word in brackets in the correct form.

1 Individuals are systematically asked to show a form of .... (identity) before being allowed to access government buildings.

2 Each piece of evidence should be presented .... (individual).

3 You will usually find .... (define) of the key terms in an essay question towards the beginning of the essay.

4 The study analyzed how children under three .... (interact) with each other in day-care settings.

5 If a teacher .... (label) a child as unintelligent at a young age, it is difficult for that child to do well in their education.

4 Match each set of words (1–5) to the words (a–e) to form collocations.

1 logical / firm / come to a
2 working / sustainable / friendly
3 deciding / key / major
4 closely / directly / strongly
5 political / literary / economic

a linked
b conclusion
c environment/environmentally
d theory
e factor

5 Complete each of these sentences with a collocation from Exercise 4.

1 He was well respected as an expert on Shakespeare and on other more modern writers, and was considered to be extremely important in the field of .... theory.

2 He lost his job, and his wife left him, but he still wasn't sure whether to move out of London – until his mother died, and that was the .... factor in his move to Lebanon.

3 The increase in deaths from lung disease was .... linked to the fact that those workers were exposed to dangerous chemicals – experts concluded that no other factors were involved.

4 It is now considered essential for companies to show themselves to be environmentally ....

5 Once you have written the main body of your essay, it is important that you .... a strong conclusion.

1 Match the words (1–10) to their definitions (a–j).

1 ambiguous
2 authority
3 culture
4 dimension
5 distribute
6 emphasis
7 global
8 occur
9 seek
10 tradition

a the legal right or ability to control

b a part or feature of something or a way of thinking about something

c the importance given to something

d to give something out or supply something

e the way of life of a group of people, especially related to traditions and beliefs

f relating to the whole world

g to look for

h having more than one possible meaning, often making meaning unclear

i the way people act or a belief that has happened for a long time

j to happen

2 Complete this table with the different forms of words from Exercise 1.

verb	noun	adjective	adverb
	1 _____	ambiguous	ambiguously
authorize	authority	2 _____ authoritative	authoritatively
	culture	3 _____	
	dimension	4 _____	dimensionally
distribute	distribution distributor	5 _____ distributed	
emphasize	6 _____	emphasized emphatic	emphatically
globalize	7 _____	global	globally
occur	occurrence	8 _____	
	tradition	9 _____	traditionally

3 Complete each of these sentences with the word in brackets in the correct form.

1 The argument put forward in the essay was rather unclear – in fact, it was rather _____ (ambiguity).

2 He was given _____ (authorize) access to the historical archives at the university.

3 One of the company's key _____ (distribute) failed to fulfil their obligations, and this was one of the factors that led to a decreased turnover.

4 The study _____ (emphasis) the connection between depression and genetics.

5 This issue is not just a domestic problem, only affecting the UK – it is now a _____ (global) issue and therefore must be taken seriously.

4 Match each set of words (1–5) to the words (a–e) to form collocations.

1 identity / differences / context
2 political / social / economic
3 frequent / rare / common
4 advice / refuge / compensation
5 old / follow a / break with

a occurrence
b cultural
c tradition
d dimension
e seek

5 Complete each of these sentences with a collocation from Exercise 4.

1 Second-generation immigrants sometimes _____ the traditions of their parents and take on Western customs instead.

2 Following an accident at work, it is likely that an employee will seek _____ , so it is necessary for companies to take out insurance so that they have enough money to cope with situations like this.

3 During the study, it was fortunate that incidents where respondents refused to co-operate were _____ occurrences.

4 It is important to recognize the cultural _____ between two companies before they merge, so that action can be taken to ensure that the merger runs as smoothly as possible.

5 There was a strong _____ dimension to the party's manifesto, as it had always promised to support the poorest and the weakest.

Unit 7

1 Match the words (1–10) to their definitions (a–j).

1 assumption
2 coherence
3 despite
4 parallel
5 perspective
6 sequence
7 similar
8 successive
9 transfer
10 vary

a something accepted as true without evidence or questioning
b event or situation happening at the same time
c the order in which events happen
d almost the same but not exactly
e the way of looking at an issue, idea or topic
f to move someone/something from one place to another
g parts fitting together in a natural way
h to be different from each other
i happening one after the other without break
j not influenced by or taking notice of something

2 Complete this table with the different forms of words from Exercise 1.

verb	noun	adjective	adverb
1	assumption	assumed	
	coherence	2	coherently
parallel	parallel	parallel	3 ....
	sequence	4	sequentially
	5	similar	similarly
succeed	6 .... success	successive	successively
transfer	7 .... transferral	transferred	
vary	variation 8	varying varied 9 .... various	varyingly 10 ....

3 Complete each of these sentences with the word in brackets in the correct form.

1 You must ensure that you develop a .... (coherence) argument in the body of your essay.

2 Two studies examining the behaviour of elephants in the wild were conducted in .... (parallel).

3 The investigation was considered to be largely .... (succeed), despite the fact that a lot of questions remained unanswered.

4 Once the new government were elected, the .... (transfer) of power was handled rather badly.

5 The entire class of students graduated from university at the end of the year with .... (vary) success.

4 Match each set of words (1–4) to the words (a–d) to form collocations.

1 logical / out of / of events
2 make the / working on the / based on the
3 broadly / roughly / remarkably
4 global / feminist / wider

a similar
b assumption
c perspective
d sequence

5 Complete each of these sentences with a collocation from Exercise 4.

1 The arguments in the report followed a structured and .... sequence.

2 When examined from a .... perspective, the novel is seen to portray women in an extremely unrealistic light.

3 Having observed the way in which discussions were run in Head Office, I wrongly .... assumption that they would be run in a similar way at all subsidiaries.

4 Whilst not identical, their work was so .... similar that it was felt they must have plagiarized.

6 Replace the words or phrases in italics with collocations from Exercise 4 in the correct form.

1 The *order of the day* was based on previous years' experience.

2 *The idea was formed* that people are largely motivated by money.

3 The idea and design of the product was not exactly new, it was *fairly close* to another company's.

4 Many companies now try to look at their products not only from a local mind set but from *an international point of view.*

7 Use words from the exercises on this page to create five sentences on the topic of this unit.

Unit 8

1 Match the words (1–10) to their definitions (a–j).

1 complementary	**a** to include or contain
2 comprise	**b** to be made of or formed from something
3 consist	
4 construct	**c** to make something available to people, especially in a book, journal or newspaper
5 contribute	
6 create	**d** to make or invent something new
7 function	**e** useful or attractive together
8 publish	**f** an economic area, such a finance
9 sector	
10 undertake	**g** to build something or put something together
	h to begin to do something
	i the purpose of something
	j to give something, such as effort or money, to achieve something together

2 Complete this table with the different forms of words from Exercise 1.

verb	noun	adjective	adverb
complement	1	complementary	
construct	2	constructed constructive	3 ....
contribute	contribution	4 .... contributing	
create	creation	5	creatively
6	function	functioning	
publish	publication	7 .... publishing publishable	
undertake	8		

3 Complete each of these sentences with the word in brackets in the correct form.

1 The ideal team consists of people with .... (*complement*) skills.

2 The recent .... (*construct*) of a new power station caused understandable concern amongst local residents.

3 Devising a successful brand image for a new company requires a great deal of .... (*create*) input.

4 The recently .... (*publish*) journal has come under a lot of criticism.

4 Match each set of words (1–5) to the words (a–e) to form collocations.

1 mainly of / entirely of / solely of

2 public / private / retail

3 perform a / fulfil a

4 towards / substantially / significantly

5 a task / a project / research

a consist

b contribute

c function

d undertake

e sector

5 Complete each of these sentences with a collocation from Exercise 4.

1 The team consisted .... staff from the Marketing and Sales departments, but there were also representatives from the Production and Logistics departments.

2 The impact of the recent bad weather on deliveries contributed .... the increase in complaints in the last two weeks.

3 The Sales Team .... their function, and therefore the product launch was considered a total success.

4 A large percentage of the British population work for the government in the .... sector.

5 The three senior scientists were asked to undertake .... into the causes of a serious condition connected to kidney failure.

6 Replace the words or phrases in italics with collocations from Exercise 4 in the correct form.

1 The company *was made up of only* five people and one product idea.

2 During the recession, *the shops have* been badly affected by customers making cuts in their spending.

3 The company *operates* between businesses by selling advertising space.

4 A healthy diet *helps lead to* an increase in life expectancy.

5 The project was divided up so that each person only had to *do* small *pieces of work*.

7 Use words from the exercises on this page to create five sentences on the topic of this unit.

Unit 9

1 Match the words (1–10) to their definitions (a–j).

1 context
2 emerge
3 ethic
4 gender
5 impact
6 investigate
7 major
8 minor
9 signify
10 sole

a accepted belief that controls behaviour

b a powerful effect, often from something new, that something has on a person or situation

c more serious, more important or bigger than other similar things

d less serious, less important or smaller than other similar things

e the situation that something exists or happens in

f to examine or look into carefully, often to try to discover the truth

g to mean or to be a sign of something

h to appear

i the only one

j social and/or physical condition of being male or female

2 Complete this table with the different forms of words from Exercise 1.

verb	noun	adjective	adverb
contextualize	context	1 _____	contextually
emerge	2 _____	emergent emerged emerging	
	ethic	3 _____	ethically
impact	impact	4 _____	
investigate	5 _____	investigative	
major	6 _____	major	
	7 _____	minor	
signify	signification 8 _____	9 _____	significantly
		sole	10 _____

3 Complete each of these sentences with the word in brackets in the correct form.

1 If students come across vocabulary in a test paper that they don't understand, they should look for _____ (*contextualize*) clues to help them understand the meaning.

2 It is not unusual for additional, unexpected findings to _____ (*emerge*) following a period of intensive research.

3 The practice of employing relatives and close associates is _____ (*ethic*) questionable.

4 The article was considered to be an amazing piece of _____ (*investigate*) journalism.

5 It has been proven that following the consumption of alcohol, reaction times are _____ (*signify*) impaired.

4 Match each set of words (1–5) to the words (a–e) to form collocations.

1 purpose / responsibility / rights
2 disaster / part / political issue
3 relatively / extremely / fairly
4 role / difference / stereotype
5 significant / minimal / direct

a impact
b major
c sole
d gender
e minor

5 Complete each of these sentences with a collocation from Exercise 4.

1 The impact of the advertising campaign was _____ , due to the fact that adverts were shown when very few people would be watching television.

2 The country's economy has suffered due to several major _____ , including an earthquake and a hurricane.

3 The contract was drawn up so that inventor has sole _____ to his ideas – they cannot be exploited by anyone else.

4 Some argue that dressing baby girls in pink is simply a response to a gender _____ , whereas others claim that females are naturally attracted to the colour pink.

5 The symptoms of this virus are _____ minor – in fact, some of the infected people hardly realized they were ill.

Unit 10

1 Match the words (1–10) to their definitions (a–j).

1 attribute	a a characteristic or quality that someone/something has
2 credit	
3 distinguish	b adult-like behaviour seen in a positive way
4 generation	
5 mature	c happening or existing before
6 overall	d people of the same age group
7 previous	e something that is possible; a person's ability to succeed
8 potential	
9 resolve	f praise or approval
10 target	g to solve a problem or difficult situation

h in general, not in particular

i an aim

j to make two things appear different; to notice the difference

2 Complete this table with the different forms of words from Exercise 1.

verb	noun	adjective	adverb
1	attribute	attributable	
credit	2	creditable	creditably
3	distinction	distinguishable distinction distinctive	distinguishably
generate	generation	4	generationally
5	maturity	mature	maturely
		previous	6 ....
	potential	7	potentially
resolve	8	resolved	
9	target	targetable 10	

3 Complete each of these sentences with the word in brackets in the correct form.

1 The falling sales figures are .... (*attribute*) to the lack of investment in marketing.

2 It was almost impossible to .... (*distinguish*) between the top two students.

3 When a country's economy is suffering, it needs to focus on the .... (*generate*) of new income as well as the cutting of costs.

4 Once the young birds reach .... (*mature*), they fly the nest and embark on their own adventures.

4 Match each set of words (1–5) to the words (a–e) to form collocations.

1 day / chapter / owner

2 sales / reach a / growth

3 have / show / realize

4 give / deserve / claim

5 a dispute / a conflict / fully

a credit

b previous

c potential

d resolve

e target

5 Complete each of these sentences with a collocation from Exercise 4.

1 It is a requirement of law that the previous .... of a house provides all legal documentation relating to the property.

2 Careful planning is necessary if any team is to .... a given target.

3 This study .... the potential to influence all future research within the field.

4 Successful managers .... credit to staff wherever it is due.

5 The president does not intend to give up until this issue is .... resolved.

6 Replace the words or phrases in italics with collocations from Exercise 4 in the correct form.

1 The deadline was *yesterday*.

2 The company set *an aim to get bigger by* 10% by the end of their five-year plan.

3 He has *demonstrated a lot of possible ability* during his short time with the firm.

4 She *should have received a lot of respect* for her efforts.

5 They had to *deal with many arguments* before they could move on.

7 Use words from the exercises on this page to create five sentences on the topic of this unit.

Unit 11

1 Match the words (1–10) to their definitions (a–j).

1	accurate	**a** the opposite
2	apparent	**b** can be seen and understood
3	contrast	**c** to discuss a topic, often in a formal way
4	converse	
5	debate	**d** the relationship between two groups or amounts
6	demonstrate	**e** to show
7	manipulate	**f** to ask people questions in order to find out opinions, behaviours, etc.
8	ratio	
9	statistic	**g** correct and exact
10	survey	**h** information from a study of the number of times something is present or happens
		i to control something or influence it unfairly
		j to compare two things to show a difference

2 Complete this table with the different forms of words from Exercise 1.

verb	noun	adjective	adverb
	1	accurate	accurately
		apparent	2 ....
contrast	contrast	3	contrastingly
	converse	4	conversely
debate	debate	debating 5 .... 6	
demonstrate	7	demonstrative	demonstratively
manipulate	manipulation	8	
	statistic	9	statistically
10	survey	surveyed	

3 Complete each of these sentences with the word in brackets in the correct form.

1 The essay asks you to compare and .... (*contrast*) two theories.

2 Although previous studies found a connection between ill health and caffeine intake, this study found the .... (*converse*) to be true.

3 The 1970s was a time of political unrest in the UK, and there were several .... (*demonstrate*) each week.

4 The way in which journalists portrayed the young actor was thought be extremely .... (*manipulate*).

5 The government report was found to be .... (*statistic*) inaccurate.

4 Match each set of words (1–5) to the words (a–e) to form collocations.

1 the … shows / conduct a / carry out a

2 heated / public / provoke

3 fairly / not strictly / completely

4 become / immediately / reason

5 high / calculate the / between

a debate

b survey

c accurate

d ratio

e apparent

5 Complete each of these sentences with a collocation from Exercise 4.

1 The survey .... that the population in the south of the country is increasing, whilst the population in the north is decreasing.

2 The decision to introduce a redundancy programme has .... a lot of debate amongst the staff.

3 Despite numerous criticisms, the researchers have maintained that their data is .... accurate.

4 The apparent .... for an increase in absenteeism was the appointment of the new team leader.

5 It is a legal requirement that the ratio .... children under two and adult supervisors is 1:3.

Unit 12

1 Match the words (1–10) to their definitions (a–j).

1 allocate
2 analyze
3 appropriate
4 contradict
5 infer
6 income
7 occupation
8 proportion
9 require
10 valid

a to look at or think about something in detail
b to form an opinion based on the information you have
c money earned
d something that is correct or good for a particular purpose
e a job
f to use for a particular purpose or give to a particular person
g an amount of something in relation to the whole
h to need something
i a good and acceptable reason or point
j to disagree with something, often to the extent of meaning the opposite.

2 Complete this table with the different forms of the words in Exercise 1.

verb	noun	adjective	adverb
allocate	1		
analyze	2	analytical	analytically
3	appropriacy	appropriate	4 ....
contradict	5	contradictory	
infer	6	inferential	inferentially
7	occupation		
proportion	proportion	8	proportionately
require	9	required	
10	validity	valid	

3 Complete each of these sentences with the word in brackets in the correct form.

1 The product suffered due to the low .... (*allocate*) of funds to its marketing campaign.

2 A detailed .... (*analyze*) of the market shows that age rather than social class is a good indication of consumer behaviour.

3 There was a .... (*contradict*) between the company's actual strategy and its intended strategy.

4 A number of .... (*infer*) can be made based on the current situation.

5 Many companies run an .... (*occupation*) health and pensions scheme.

4 Match each set of words (1–5) to the words (a–e) to form collocations.

1 reason / argument / criticism
2 household / family / disposable
3 highly / entirely / wholly
4 surplus to / legal / satisfy
5 high / large / small

a income
b appropriate
c valid
d requirements
e proportion

5 Complete each of these sentences with a collocation from Exercise 4. In one case, several answers are possible.

1 It was not considered a valid .... for the failure.

2 An increase in .... income is particularly beneficial to retailers of luxury goods.

3 Her grades did not .... the entry requirements.

4 Only a .... proportion of people – 1 in 100 – responded to the survey.

5 The presentation was .... appropriate given the change in the market.

6 Replace the words or phrases in italics with collocations from Exercise 4 in the correct form.

1 He failed to meet the deadline and did not have a *good enough excuse* for doing so.

2 *The domestic money* is used as a measure of living standards in a country.

3 Many technological innovations are eventually *no longer needed*.

4 *The biggest group* of people working for the company come from an accounting background.

7 Which two words from the collocations *highly/entirely/wholly appropriate* are the most similar in meaning?

8 Use words from the exercises on this page to create five sentences on the topic of this unit.

The Academic Word List

abandon
abstract
academy
access
accommodate
accompany
accumulate
accurate
achieve
acknowledge
acquire
adapt
adequate
adjacent
adjust
administrate
adult
advocate
affect
aggregate
aid
albeit
allocate
alter
alternative
ambiguous
amend
analogy
analyze
annual
anticipate
apparent
append
appreciate
approach
appropriate
approximate
arbitrary
area
aspect
assemble
assess
assign
assist
assume

assure
attach
attain
attitude
attribute
author
authority
automate
available
aware

behalf
benefit
bias
bond
brief
bulk

capable
capacity
category
cease
challenge
channel
chapter
chart
chemical
circumstance
cite
civil
clarify
classic
clause
code
coherent
coincide
collapse
colleague
commence
comment
commission
commit
commodity
communicate
community

compatible
compensate
compile
complement
complex
component
compound
comprehensive
comprise
compute
conceive
concentrate
concept
conclude
concurrent
conduct
confer
confine
confirm
conflict
conform
consent
consequent
considerable
consist
constant
constitute
constrain
construct
consult
consume
contact
contemporary
context
contract
contradict
contrary
contrast
contribute
controversy
convene
converse
convert
convince
cooperate
coordinate
core
corporate
correspond
couple

create
credit
criteria
crucial
culture
currency
cycle

data
debate
decade
decline
deduce
define
definite
demonstrate
denote
deny
depress
derive
design
despite
detect
deviate
device
devote
differentiate
dimension
diminish
discrete
discriminate
displace
display
dispose
distinct
distort
distribute
diverse
document
domain
domestic
dominate
draft
drama
duration
dynamic

economy
edit
element

eliminate
emerge
emphasis
empirical
enable
encounter
energy
enforce
enhance
enormous
ensure
entity
environment
equate
equip
equivalent
erode
error
establish
estate
estimate
ethic
ethnic
evaluate
eventual
evident
evolve
exceed
exclude
exhibit
expand
expert
explicit
exploit
export
expose
external
extract

facilitate
factor
feature
federal
fee
file
final
finance
finite
flexible
fluctuate

focus
format
formula
forthcoming
found
foundation
framework
function
fund
fundamental
furthermore

gender
generate
generation
globe
goal
grade
grant
guarantee
guideline

hence
hierarchy
highlight
hypothesis

identical
identify
ideology
ignorant
illustrate
image
immigrate
impact
implement
implicate
implicit
imply
impose
incentive
incidence
incline
income
incorporate
index
indicate
individual
induce
inevitable

infer
infrastructure
inherent
inhibit
initial
initiate
injure
innovate
input
insert
insight
inspect
instance
institute
instruct
integral
integrate
integrity
intelligent
intense
interact
intermediate
internal
interpret
interval
intervene
intrinsic
invest
investigate
invoke
involve
isolate
issue
item

job
journal
justify

label
labour
layer
lecture
legal
legislate
levy
liberal
licence
likewise
link

locate
logic

maintain
major
manipulate
manual
margin
mature
maximize
mechanism
media
mediate
medical
medium
mental
method
migrate
military
minimal
minimize
minimum
ministry
minor
mode
modify
monitor
motive
mutual

negate
network
neutral
nevertheless
nonetheless
norm
normal
notion
notwithstanding
nuclear

objective
obtain
obvious
occupy
occur
odd
offset
ongoing
option

orient
outcome
output
overall
overlap
overseas

panel
paradigm
paragraph
parallel
parameter
participate
partner
passive
perceive
percent
period
persist
perspective
phase
phenomenon
philosophy
physical
plus
policy
portion
pose
positive
potential
practitioner
precede
precise
predict
predominant
preliminary
presume
previous
primary
prime
principal
principle
prior
priority
proceed
process
professional
prohibit
project
promote

proportion
prospect
protocol
psychology
publication
publish
purchase
pursue

qualitative
quote

radical
random
range
ratio
rational
react
recover
refine
regime
region
register
regulate
reinforce
reject
relax
release
relevant
reluctance
rely
remove
require
research
reside
resolve
resource
respond
restore
restrain
restrict
retain
reveal
revenue
reverse
revise
revolution
rigid
role
route

scenario
schedule
scheme
scope
section
sector
secure
seek
select
sequence
series
sex
shift
significant
similar
simulate
site
so-called
sole
somewhat
source
specific
specify
sphere
stable
statistic
status
straightforward
strategy
stress
structure
style
submit
subordinate
subsequent
subsidy
substitute
successor
sufficient
sum
summary
supplement
survey
survive
suspend
sustain
symbol

tape
target

task
team
technical
technique
technology
temporary
tense
terminate
text
theme
theory
thereby
thesis
topic
trace
tradition
transfer
transform
transit
transmit
transport
trend
trigger

ultimate
undergo
underlie
undertake
uniform
unify
unique
utilize

valid
vary
vehicle
version
via
violate
virtual
visible
vision
visual
volume
voluntary

welfare
whereas
whereby
widespread